George W. Bush

George W. Bush

Matt Donnelly

Children's Press®
A Division of Scholastic Inc.
New York / Toronto / London / Auckland / Sydney
Mexico City / New Delhi / Hong Kong
Danbury, Connecticut

Library of Congress Cataloging-in-Publication Data

Donnelly, Matt, 1972–
George W. Bush / Matt Donnelly.
p. cm. — (Encyclopedia of presidents. Second series)
Includes bibliographical references (p.) and index.
ISBN 0-516-22972-9
1. Bush, George W. (George Walker), 1946– —Juvenile literature. 2. Presidents—United States—Biography—Juvenile literature. I. Title. II. Series: Encyclopedia of presidents (2003).

E903.D66 2005
973.931'092—dc22 2004020187

 Published in 2005 by Children's Press, an imprint of Scholastic Library Publishing.
Published simultaneously in Canada.
Printed in the United States of America.

1 2 3 4 5 6 7 8 9 10 R 14 13 12 11 10 09 08 07 06 05

Contents

Chapter 1

America Attacked

Terror in the Skies

Minutes after American Airlines Flight 11 took off from Boston on its way to Los Angeles, passengers heard an unknown voice broadcasting from the cockpit.

"We have some planes. Just stay quiet and you'll be OK. We are returning to the airport. Nobody move. Everything will be OK. If you try to make any moves, you'll endanger yourself and the airplane. Just stay quiet."

The time was 8:24 a.m. on September 11, 2001, and the voice belonged to Mohamed Atta, a trained pilot and a *terrorist* (a person using extreme acts of violence to make a political statement). Atta was at the controls, and three or four other terrorists were in the passenger cabin. In gaining control of the plane, they had stabbed two flight attendants, a passenger, the pilot, and the copilot. Now they threatened other passengers with Mace, pepper spray, and a bomb.

Atta was not returning to the airport. Instead, he was headed toward New York City. At 8:44 a.m., a flight attendant reported on her cell phone, “Something is wrong. We are in a rapid descent . . . we are all over the place.” Moments later she said, “We are flying low. We are flying very, very low. We are flying way too low.” The last thing she said was, “Oh my God, we are way too low.”

Her phone went dead. About two minutes later, the plane crashed into the North Tower of the World Trade Center in New York City. The time of impact was 8:46 a.m.

“We’re at War”

Fifteen minutes later, just after 9 a.m., a limousine carrying President George W. Bush pulled up to Emma E. Booker Elementary School in Sarasota, Florida. His party had already received news that a plane had crashed into World Trade Center, but for the moment it appeared to be a tragic accident. A few minutes later, President Bush was listening to second-grade students take turns reading to him. His chief of staff, Andrew Card, leaned over to Bush and whispered chilling words into the president’s ear: “A second plane hit the second tower. America is under attack.” United Airlines Flight 175, also headed from Boston to Los Angeles, had just crashed into the South Tower of the World Trade Center.

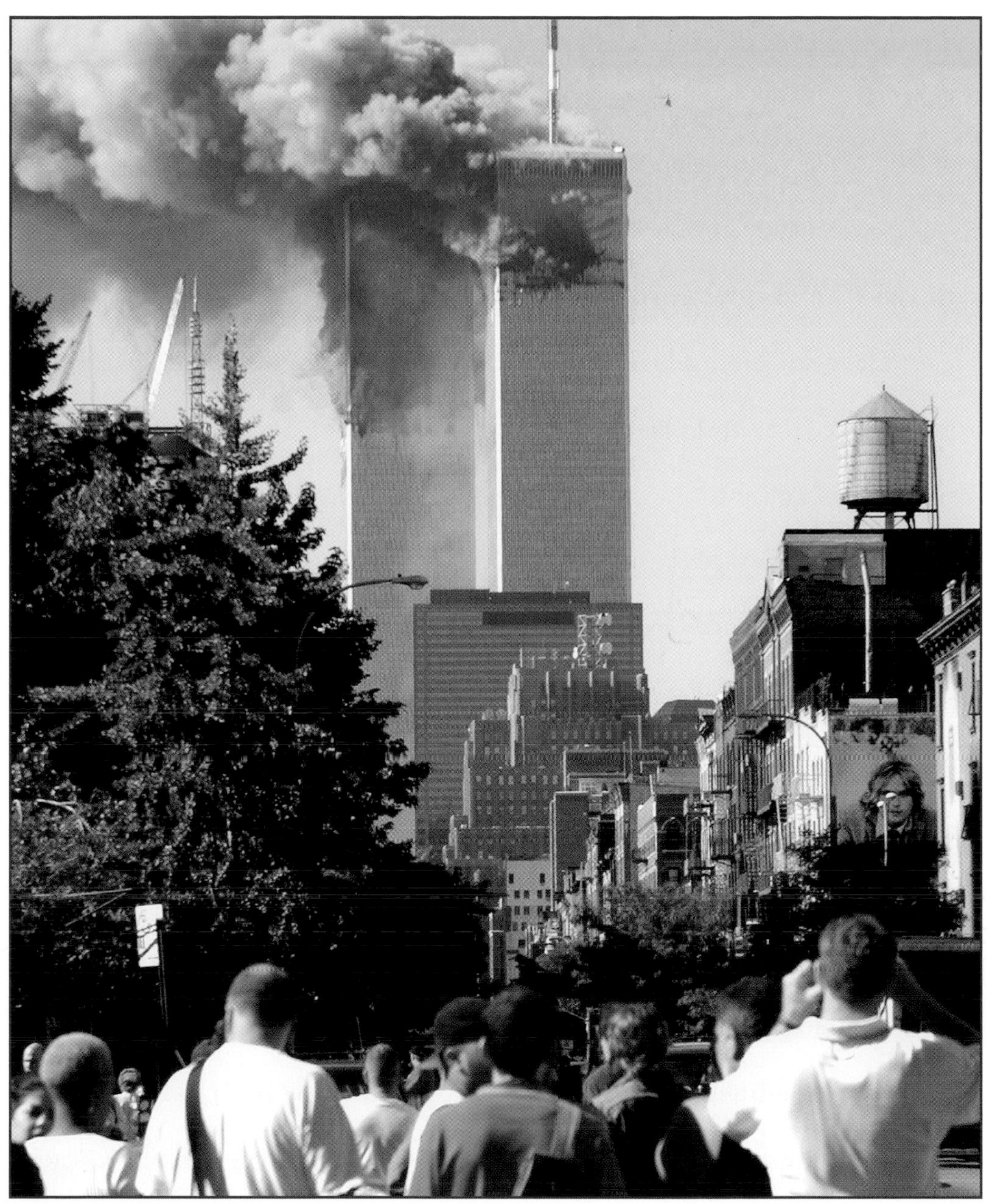

The World Trade Center towers in New York City burn after they were hit by hijacked airliners on September 11, 2001. Within hours both towers collapsed.

President Bush's face turned ashen as he heard the news. He did not want to startle the children, however, so he finished listening to the students' story. He thanked the teacher and left the classroom. In the grade-school hallway, Bush and his aides watched television images of the attacks, now believed to be the work of terrorists. "We're at war," Bush said.

The president made a brief statement to the press, then was hurried to the airport where *Air Force One* awaited. In the meantime, Secret Service agents in Washington went into action to protect other high government officers and the president's family. Vice President Richard Cheney was taken to the underground Presidential Emergency Operations Center, where he could stay in radio contact with President Bush. The president's wife Laura and his two daughters (then college students) were also taken to secure locations.

Even before the president's plane took off from Florida, there was more bad news. A third hijacked plane had crashed into the Pentagon, the headquarters of the U.S. military command, just outside of Washington, D.C. On the advice of security and military advisers, the president's plane did not return to Washington, but flew westward to Barksdale Air Force Base, in Louisiana. No one could be sure how many hijacked planes there were or what other targets might be struck.

At 10:03, a fourth hijacked plane crashed in a field in Shanksville, Pennsylvania. The plane had been heading toward Washington, D.C. Investigators

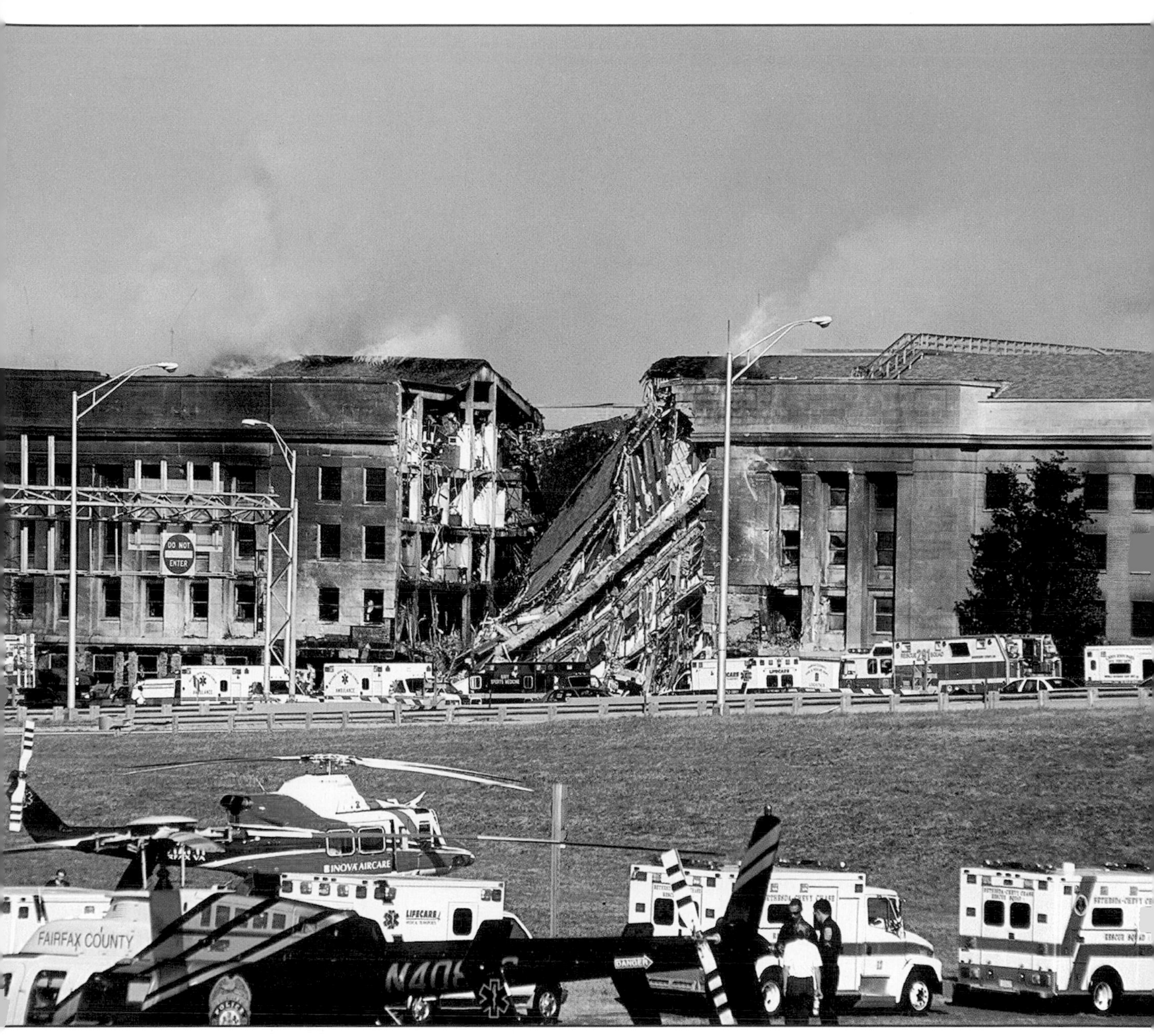

The western face of the Pentagon in Arlington, Virginia, after it was struck by a hijacked airliner on September 11. The Pentagon is the headquarters of the U.S. Defense Department.

believe the hijackers planned to crash it into the White House or the U.S. Capitol. Their plans were disrupted when passengers onboard heard about the earlier hijackings and decided to revolt against their captors, forcing the al-Qaeda pilot to crash the plane in open countryside. This turned out to be the last of the planes hijacked in an elaborate terrorist plan to express outrage and hatred for America.

In New York, the tragedy was still playing itself out. Thousands of workers had escaped from the 107-story buildings since the Twin Towers were struck by the jumbo jets. Those in floors above the crash sites were trapped amid raging fires and dense smoke. Then, shortly after 10 a.m., the South Tower collapsed, sending debris and dust in all directions. Hundreds died, including many firefighters and police officers still trying to rescue victims. Half an hour later, the North Tower also collapsed.

Leading a Nation

President Bush ordered all airplanes in the United States grounded in case other hijackings were planned. In New York and Washington, thousands of safety officers and volunteers began the horrendous job of seeking survivors at the crash sites. That afternoon, on the president's orders, *Air Force One* headed back to Washington. That evening, the president addressed the American people from the Oval Office in the White House. "This is a day when all Americans from every

President George W. Bush addresses the nation from the Oval Office on the evening of September 11. "Freedom itself has been attacked this morning," he said.

walk of life unite in our resolve for justice and peace," he said. "America has stood down enemies before, and we will do so this time." He mourned the loss of life and vowed to bring the guilty to justice. More than 3,000 people had died at the hands of terrorists on a single day.

For George W. Bush, the attacks of September 11, 2001, marked a sudden change of direction. They transformed a peacetime presidency, concerned with domestic matters such as tax reductions and energy policy, into a wartime presidency concerned with combatting international terrorism. The president himself showed a renewed sense of purpose, coming to believe that God had chosen him to lead the nation in addressing the terrorist challenge.

The Bush Pedigree

George W. Bush grew up in one of America's most privileged families. His great-grandfather, Samuel Prescott Bush, made millions in the steel business in the early 1900s and became a close adviser of President Herbert Hoover (1929–1933). His grandfather, Prescott "Pres" Bush, became a leading investment banker in New York City and served as U.S. senator from Connecticut (1952–1962). George W. Bush's father, George Herbert Walker Bush, would serve eight years as vice president (1981–1989) and four years as president of the United States (1989–1993).

Prescott and Dorothy Walker Bush, the parents of one president and the grandparents of President George W. Bush. Prescott Bush served as a U.S. senator from Connecticut.

In 1942, George H. W. Bush had passed up college to enter the U.S. Navy during World War II. He became the youngest fighter pilot in the navy and survived the destruction of his plane during an attack against a Japanese port in the Pacific. At the end of the war in 1945, the elder Bush married Barbara Pierce and entered Yale University as a freshman. Their first son, George Walker Bush, was born July 6, 1946, in New Haven, Connecticut.

After graduating from Yale in 1948, the elder George Bush moved his family to Odessa, Texas, where he entered the oil business, starting as a young assistant in a small company owned by a Bush family friend. After a year, the family moved to California, where young George's sister Robin was born. Then in 1950, the family returned to Texas, settling in Midland, 20 miles (32 kilometers) east of Odessa. They lived on West Ohio Street in a modest house painted robin's-egg blue.

Life in Midland

Midland sits on an underground reservoir of oil that covers 100,000 square miles (260,000 square kilometers). In the 1950s, however, no one yet knew exactly where the oil was. Dozens of companies were gaining mineral rights from landowners and sinking test wells, hoping for a big strike. George H. W. Bush set up a small oil company with some of his neighbors in Midland. While the Bushes

The Bush families in 1948. From left to right, Barbara Bush, toddler George W. in red cowboy boots, George H. W. Bush, Dorothy and Prescott Bush.

lived there, young George and Robin were joined by three brothers, Jeb, Neil, and Marvin. Later, after they moved to Houston, the Bushes had a second daughter, Dorothy.

Midland, a town of about 22,000 in 1950, left an indelible mark on the future president. As George W. recalled:

> We learned to respect our elders, to do what they said, and to be good neighbors. We went to church. Families spent time together, outside, the grown-ups talking with neighbors while the kids played ball or with marbles and yo-yos. Our homework and schoolwork were important. . . . No one locked their doors, because you could trust your friends and neighbors. It was a happy childhood. I was surrounded by love and friends and sports.

Young George's real love was baseball. He grew up looking at photos of the Yale team on which his father was first baseman and captain. That team had progressed to the College World Series two years in a row. Young George was soon following major league baseball as well. He traded baseball cards by the hour and sent cards to Mickey Mantle and Willie Mays to get their autographs. "I never dreamed about being president," George later said. "I wanted to be Willie Mays." Bush and his friends also spent long hours playing the game. George turned out not to be very talented, but he later said that his happiest childhood memory was playing for his father on a Midland Little League team.

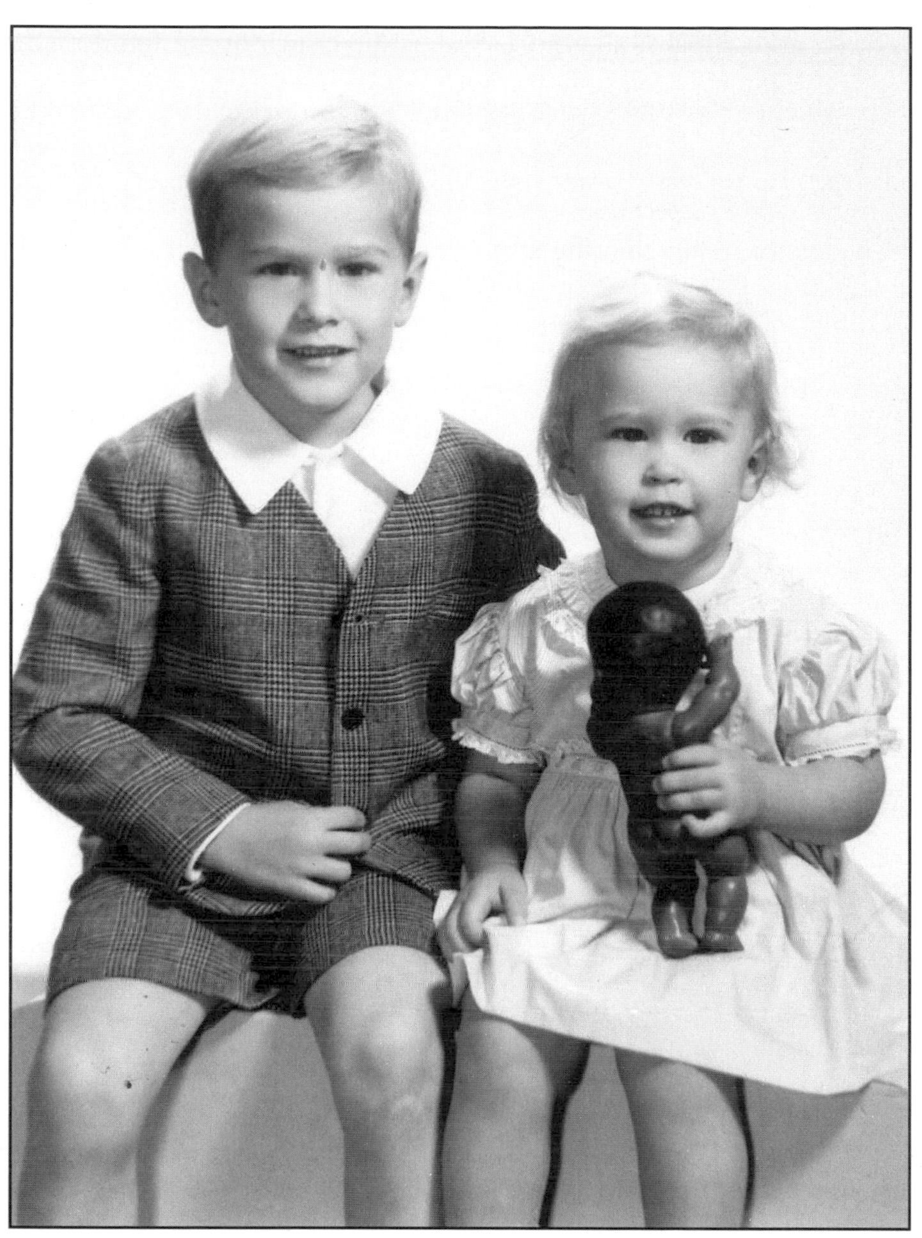

George and Robin Bush. Robin died of leukemia at the age of three in 1953.

From an early age, George served as the clown of the family. This was especially true after his three-year-old sister Robin died in 1953 of leukemia, a blood disease. He was only seven years old, but he saw his mother's sadness, and he did whatever he could to bring a smile to her face.

Young George was not particularly interested in school, and sometimes he ran into trouble at Sam Houston Elementary. Once his fourth-grade teacher dragged him to the principal's office because he was drawing whiskers and sideburns on his face with a pen. The principal immediately had George bend over, then gave the boy three hard blows with a wooden paddle. "When I hit him, he cried," the principal recalled. "Oh, did he cry! He yelled as if he'd been shot."

In seventh grade George got his first taste of politics when he ran for class president against Jack Hanks. Classmates say that George won a narrow victory purely on the strength of his personality. If the Bushes had stayed in Midland, young George might have won many other class offices there, but at the end of his seventh-grade year, his family moved from isolated Midland to Houston, the biggest city in Texas.

Chapter 2

A Charmed Life

Leaving Midland

In 1959 George's father took charge of a company that was drilling for oil underwater in the Gulf of Mexico. The family moved to Houston to be closer to the huge offshore rigs. Young George was enrolled for eighth grade at the Kincaid School, a private school in Houston. For the first time, he had to adapt to a new school and very different surroundings.

Two years later, George moved again, this time without his family. In the fall of 1961 he arrived at Phillips Academy in Andover, Massachusetts, the exclusive preparatory school where his father had studied nearly 25 years earlier. (The academy is usually known as Andover to distinguish it from another Phillips Academy in Exeter, New Hampshire.)

George soon learned that his father's academic and athletic accomplishments at Andover cast a long shadow. Some older teachers still remembered his father, and a photograph of George H. W. in his baseball uniform was prominently displayed on the campus. George realized that he would not outshine his father as an athlete or a student. Instead, he gained the admiration of his fellow students by subtly undermining the school's strict dress code. After a brief tryout with the football team, he became a leader of the cheerleading squad.

In the fall of 1963, when George was a senior at Andover, his father announced that he would run for the U.S. Senate in Texas in the 1964 elections. That November, President John F. Kennedy visited Texas, hoping to settle disputes in the Texas Democratic party. On November 22, while riding in a motorcade in Dallas, Kennedy was shot by an assassin and died soon afterward.

The American people, including most students at Andover, were shocked and horrified at news of Kennedy's *assassination*. An Andover student remembered later that the event didn't seem to affect Bush, recalling that "he just kept breezing right along the way he always did when the rest of us were staggering around in a daze like the rest of the country." Bush friends suggest that this behavior echoes the seven-year-old George trying to cheer up his mother after the tragedy of his sister's death.

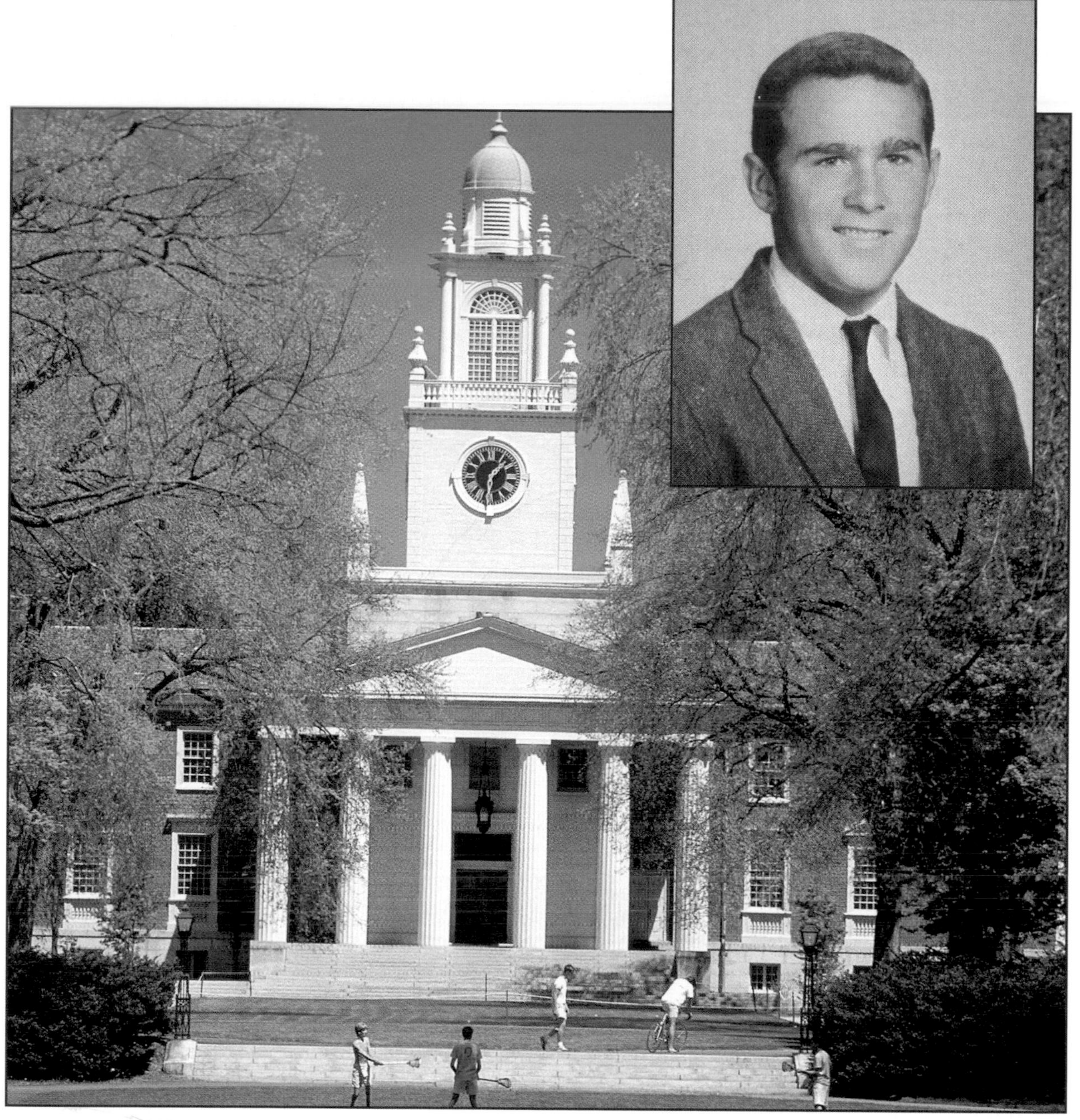

A campus building at Phillips Academy in Andover, Massachusetts. Inset, George W. Bush as a senior in the 1964 Andover yearbook.

Yale

That fall, George was also working on college applications. He wanted to attend Yale, but his academic record was far from inspiring. His guidance counselor suggested that he also apply to the University of Texas, where he might have a better chance of admission. Bush applied to both schools, and was pleased when he was accepted to Yale. It didn't hurt his chances that both his grandfather (recently a senator from Yale's home state of Connecticut) and his father (a Yale sports hero) were both Yale graduates.

The 1964 elections were a disaster for Republicans across the country, including George H. W. Bush. In the presidential race, Democratic president Lyndon Johnson defeated Republican Barry Goldwater in a landslide. In Texas, George H. W. Bush had campaigned hard for Goldwater even as he ran for the U.S. Senate against liberal senator Ralph Yarborough. President Johnson, a popular and powerful Texan himself, supported Yarborough, who gained re-election. The loss was a serious blow to Bush's political ambitions.

Young George Bush also found his father's loss difficult to accept. He mentioned this to Yale's campus pastor, the Reverend William Sloane Coffin. George knew that Coffin had known his father during their college years, but may not have known that Coffin was an activist in liberal and Democratic causes. Coffin replied, "Oh, yes. I know your father. Frankly, he was beaten by a better man."

Bush on the baseball field at Yale. He was not a great athlete or a great student, but he was known and liked by many.

George found the pastor's comment insensitive and offensive. It fed his growing resentment of the Eastern intellectual elites, who strongly favored liberal causes. He found that he identified more closely with the conservative values of the Southwest. "What angered me was the way such people at Yale felt so intellectually superior and so righteous," Bush said. "They thought they had all the answers."

George majored in history at Yale, but he spent most of his time and energy on activities outside the classroom. He joined a fraternity that included many Yale athletes, and he felt at home even though he himself was not playing a varsity sport. He enjoyed many friendships and many parties. In a commencement speech to Yale graduates in 2001, Bush remarked wryly, "As a student, I tried to keep a low profile. It worked." One friend agreed: "More than anything, George was a student of people, not subjects."

After his sophomore year at Yale, Bush spent the summer of 1966 in Texas working on his father's campaign for a seat in the U.S. House of Representatives. In November, Bush Senior won the seat. During his visits to Texas, young George had also developed a serious romance with Cathy Wolfman, a bright and outgoing student at Rice University in Houston. In December the couple announced their engagement. "He was kind, caring, and sensitive. And he used to make me laugh all the time," Cathy said. At first the wedding was scheduled for the summer of

The Bush family in 1966. Young George (third from right) was between his sophomore and junior years at Yale.

1967, then it was postponed to the following year. Living and studying 2,000 miles (3,200 km) from each other, George and Cathy were nagged by second thoughts. Finally Cathy returned her engagement ring and ended the relationship. George was devastated.

As George entered his senior year at Yale, opposition to the Vietnam War was growing rapidly, especially on college campuses. Yale and many other universities saw major campus demonstrations and disruptions. Bush did not join the protesters, and he seemed to support the actions of the United States in the war.

The Vietnam War

Vietnam, long a colony of France, occupies one side of a long peninsula facing the South China Sea. After the French gave up control of the region in the 1950s, it was divided between a *Communist* government (a system in which the government owns and manages all property and business) in the north and a democratic government supported by Western nations (including the United States) in the south.

In the late 1950s, Communist guerrilla fighters known as the Vietcong began attacking towns and cities in South Vietnam. They hoped to persuade the people of the south to support a united Vietnam under Communist rule. The United States supplied military advice and supplies to South Vietnam, but the fighting continued. In 1965 American ground troops joined the battle. In the next three years, the number of U.S. combatants increased to more than 500,000. The Vietcong, now supported by regular North Vietnamese troops, continued to attack.

During the 1960s, the U.S. armed services relied both on volunteers and on the *draft*, a system in which the government could call up able-bodied young men for military service. The draft system offered many deferments (exemptions for college study, marriage, and the like). As U.S. involvement in Vietnam increased, however, many more men were drafted and many deferments were ended.

Like many others his age, however, he did not welcome the prospect of being drafted into the military to serve in Southeast Asia.

Serving His Country

Like many other young men during the 1960s, Bush found a compromise that involved serving in the military but avoiding combat duty in Vietnam. Through the influence of family friends, he gained permission to apply for a place in the Texas Air National Guard, jumping to the top of a long waiting list. In January 1968, he took the Air Force Officer Qualifying Test. He scored in the top 5 percent on the "officer quality" section and just passed the pilot/navigator section.

On May 28, 1968, a week before his graduation from Yale, Bush flew to Houston to enlist for a six-year term in the 147th Fighter-Interceptor Group of the Texas Air National Guard. He told the commander of the 147th that he wanted to become a fighter pilot as his father had been in World War II, but on an application question about overseas service, he checked the box "do not volunteer." He was accepted into the pilot trainee program.

In July 1968, Bush began six weeks of airman's basic training and was commissioned as a second lieutenant. Later, he attended flight school at Moody Air Force Base in Georgia, graduating in November 1969. Returning to Texas in December, he trained to be an F-102A pilot and was certified in June 1970. From

Bush in the Texas Air National Guard. He enlisted for six years of part-time and weekend duty.

June 1970 to April 1972, he flew training missions once or twice a month. Altogether, between 1968 and 1972 he served the equivalent of 21 months of active duty.

In May 1972, Bush asked to be transferred temporarily to Alabama so that he could work in the Senate campaign of Republican Winton Blount. Bush's father, concerned that young George was still adrift in life, with no particular goals or plans, had helped arrange the campaign assignment. Blount lost the election in November, and Bush returned to Houston.

A Dose of Humility

In December 1972, Bush visited his family in Washington, where his father was serving in the House of Representatives. One night young George got drunk, crashed his car into a neighbor's trash cans, and woke up the entire neighborhood, including his father. George Senior first encountered 18-year-old Jeb and told him to bring George to the den for a chat.

Young George was in a fighting mood and challenged his father to a fight. Shaking his fist, he said, "You wanna go *mano a mano* right here?"

As George Senior stood up to meet his son, Jeb Bush stepped between them. "Hey, everybody," he said. "Guess what? George has been accepted into Harvard Business School."

Still in a fighting mood, George said, "I'm not going. I just wanted to let you know that I could get in."

George Senior was deeply concerned about his son's future. George W. was 26 years old and had little sense of direction. When George Senior was 26, he already had a family and a career. Through friends, Congressman Bush arranged for young George to take a volunteer position at a social services program in a poor Houston neighborhood. Called Professionals United for Leadership League (PULL), it was managed by professional football players and other athletes to mentor black children from underprivileged backgrounds. To the surprise of many, including members of his own family, George was a natural. He played basketball with the kids and tried hard to be just like anyone else on the staff. George forged a special bond with a seven-year-old named Jimmy Dean. "He was an adorable kid," said a PULL staff member. "Everybody liked him, but he bypassed all these famous athletes, all these giants, and picked out George Bush, and vice versa." George later said, "He was like my adopted little brother."

During 1973, George continued his Texas National Guard responsibilities. U.S. involvement in Vietnam had been diminishing rapidly, and all troops were withdrawn in the spring of 1973. Later that year, Bush received formal permission to end his active guard duty eight months short of the full six-year term in order to enroll at the Harvard Business School. He received an honorable discharge on October 2, 1973.

Harvard Business School

The Harvard Business School was one of the most respected schools of its kind in the nation. Many of its classes were taught using "case studies," actual business problems that students were expected to solve. Class participation and teamwork were encouraged. George's grades were mediocre, but he often directed class discussions and became a team leader. Later George wrote that Harvard "gave me the tools and the vocabulary of the business world."

George came to Harvard with a chip on his shoulder. Still suspicious of Eastern elites, he insisted on identifying himself as a Westerner in dress and behavior. "One of my first recollections of him," said one classmate, "was sitting in class and hearing the unmistakable sound of someone spitting tobacco. I turned around and there was George sitting in the back of the room in his bomber jacket spitting in a cup. You have to remember this was Harvard Business School. You just didn't see that kind of thing."

Outside of class, Bush took up jogging along the banks of the Charles River, which separated Harvard and its surroundings from Boston. He still bristled at the snobbery of the Harvard elite, but at least he and his classmates agreed

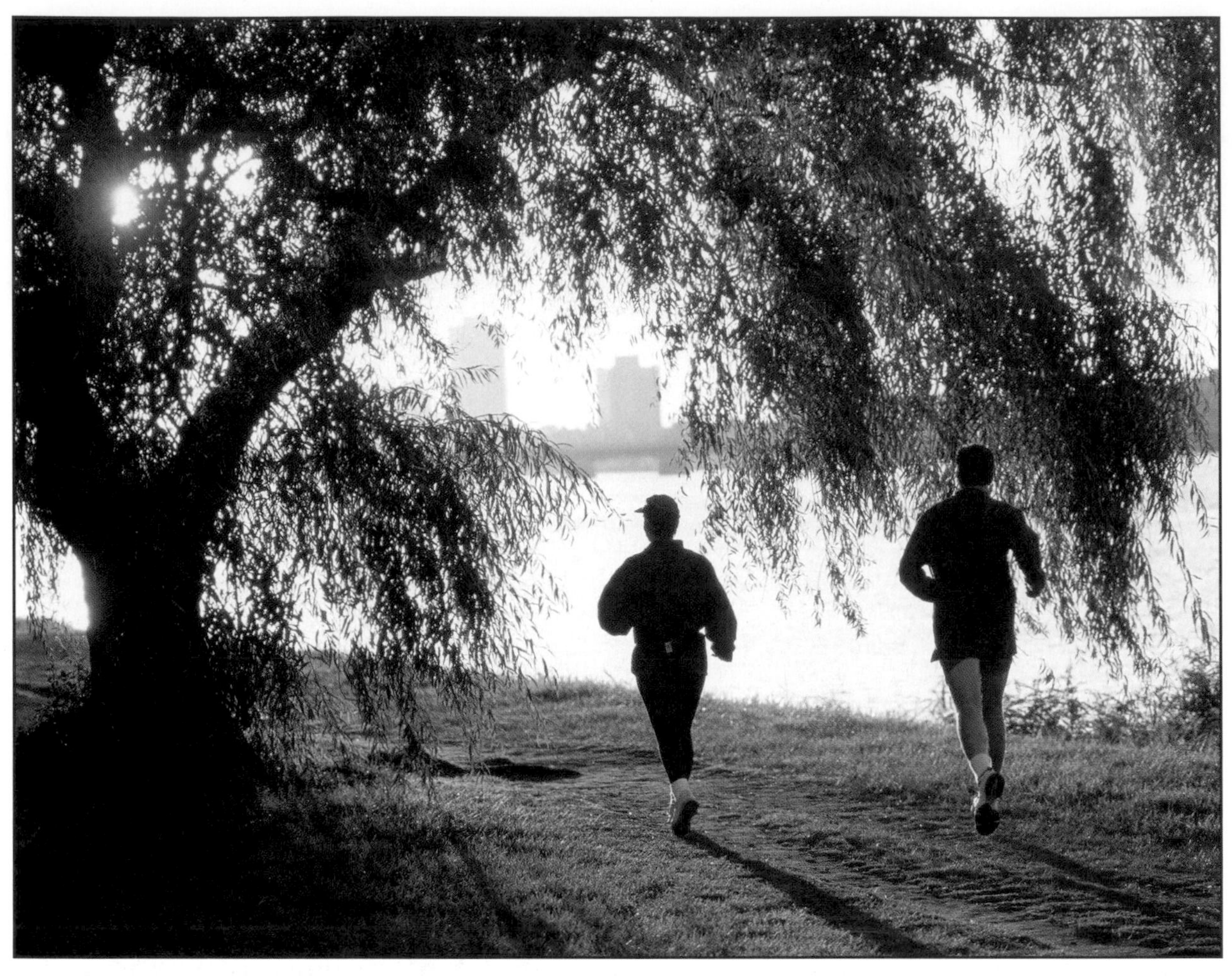

As a student at the Harvard Business School, Bush often jogged along the Esplanade, a park along the Charles River, which runs between Cambridge and Boston.

about the importance of business values. While he didn't win any prizes for his class work, he followed through and graduated in the spring of 1975. His mother, Barbara Bush, thought his years at the business school were important. "Harvard

A Father on the Rise

As young George Bush drifted from college to Texas and then to Harvard, his father was moving from one influential post to another. In 1970, he made a second run for the U.S. Senate in Texas, but he lost once again. Soon afterward, President Richard Nixon appointed him the chief U.S. representative to the United Nations. Late in 1972, he became chairman of the Republican National Committee. There he had the painful task of defending the president against growing evidence of wrongdoing in the Watergate scandal. By August 1974, Nixon was facing impeachment charges and almost certain removal from office. Nixon chose instead to resign. His vice president, Gerald Ford, was sworn in as president.

Just before young George Bush returned for his second year at Harvard in 1974, his father was in the news once again. President Ford appointed George H. W. Bush chief U.S. liaison officer to China.

Bush's parents in Beijing, China, in 1974, when George H. W. Bush was serving as chief U.S. liaison to the People's Republic of China.

was a great turning point for him," she said. "I don't think he'd say that as much as I would. I think he learned—what's that word?—structure."

Most of the students in Bush's business school class were lining up jobs on Wall Street, the center of the financial world in New York City. George Bush was headed in a different direction. Supported by a Harvard Business School study showing high-paying jobs in the oil business and his family's history in the business, his choice became clear. He packed up his 1970 Oldsmobile Cutlass and made the long drive home to Texas. Later George said that he felt he needed to answer "the entrepreneurial call I felt in my soul."

Chapter 3

Coming Into His Own

Starting Over

When 29-year-old George W. Bush returned to Texas, he didn't settle in Houston. Instead, he returned to Midland, the small city in West Texas where he had spent his boyhood. He also didn't apply for junior executive positions suitable for a business school graduate. Instead, he took a $100-per-day job as a freelance oil and mineral record researcher. This helped him to learn the oil business from the bottom up. Despite his initial lack of knowledge, he was convinced that success would be just a matter of time.

He could afford to ease into the business. "I was single," he remembered. "My overhead was extremely low." He rented a two-room apartment from family friends and soon turned it into a pigsty. "His apartment was a disaster area," said a friend. "It looked like a toxic waste dump." His clothes were a mess, and he wore Chinese slippers everywhere he went, even to business conferences. When his dirty clothes piled up high enough, he asked wives of friends to wash them for him. Friends took pity on George by giving him their old clothes. Yet he still attracted a steady stream of girlfriends.

At first Bush found it difficult to get a start in the real oil business. Even though he had spent his boyhood there, his family moved away from Midland when he was 13. He had few friendships and fewer business connections. As one of his Midland friends later recalled, "He was viewed as an outsider. . . . Back then, to the few people who knew who he was, he was just a rich Yankee kid."

Driving Drunk

Despite his new start in Texas, George continued his reckless lifestyle. His heavy drinking continued, and he often drove drunk. In September 1976, when he was in Maine visiting his family, he was arrested for drunk driving. Appearing briefly in court four days later, he pleaded guilty and paid a $150 fine. He lost his Maine driving privileges for a month.

The arrest, reported in the local press, was a great embarrassment to the Bush family. George's father was now the director of the Central Intelligence Agency, one of America's most important intelligence organizations. As he had done a few years earlier, George H. W. Bush scolded his son. "You're not a kid anymore," he said. "This is a wake-up call. You're thirty years old. It's time to start acting responsibly and cut back on your drinking." This time, young George's response was shame rather than anger.

When Bush returned to Midland, he mulled over his father's words. He knew it was time to become a responsible adult. By June 1977, George had raised funds from Bush family friends and set up his own oil exploration company. He named it Arbusto, the Spanish word for "bush." Many of the early wells Arbusto drilled were dry, but its performance would gradually improve. Meanwhile, George W. Bush had become a businessman with his own company.

Lovely Laura

Soon after Arbusto was formed, Bush learned that the local Texas congressman was retiring. In July 1977, George announced that he would be a candidate for the congressional seat in the 1978 election. With this public pronouncement, he began his political career.

The following month, in August 1977, George attended a backyard barbeque hosted by Joe and Jan O'Neill. The O'Neills introduced him to another of their single friends, Laura Welch. Laura, a librarian in Austin, the state capital, was visiting her parents in Midland. She had grown up there, only twelve blocks from the Bush family, and had been in the same junior high school class as

George. She was the daughter of Harold Bruce Welch, a successful real estate developer. Nicknamed "Lovely Laura" by her friends, she had been a cheerleader and an excellent student at Southern Methodist University in Houston. George and Laura discovered that they had even lived in the same Houston apartment complex for a few months after college.

"I don't know that it was love at first sight," Laura said later. "But it was close." George recalled that Laura was "gorgeous, good-humored, quick to laugh, down-to-earth, and very smart. I recognized those attributes right away, in roughly that order." She was a good listener, and he was a big talker. When he told joke after joke, she laughed and laughed. George was funny and outgoing, just like Laura's father. They talked until midnight. For the next three weeks they saw each other often while Laura was still in Midland. When she returned to Austin, they talked often by phone. Soon George asked Laura to marry him.

"I think it was a whirlwind romance because we were both in our early thirties," Laura said. "I'm sure both of us thought, 'Gosh, we may never get married.' And we both really wanted children. Plus, I lived in Austin and he lived in Midland, so if we were going to see each other all the time, we needed to marry." The news came as a shock and then a relief to George's parents. Having met a number of George's earlier girlfriends, they took to Laura right away. On

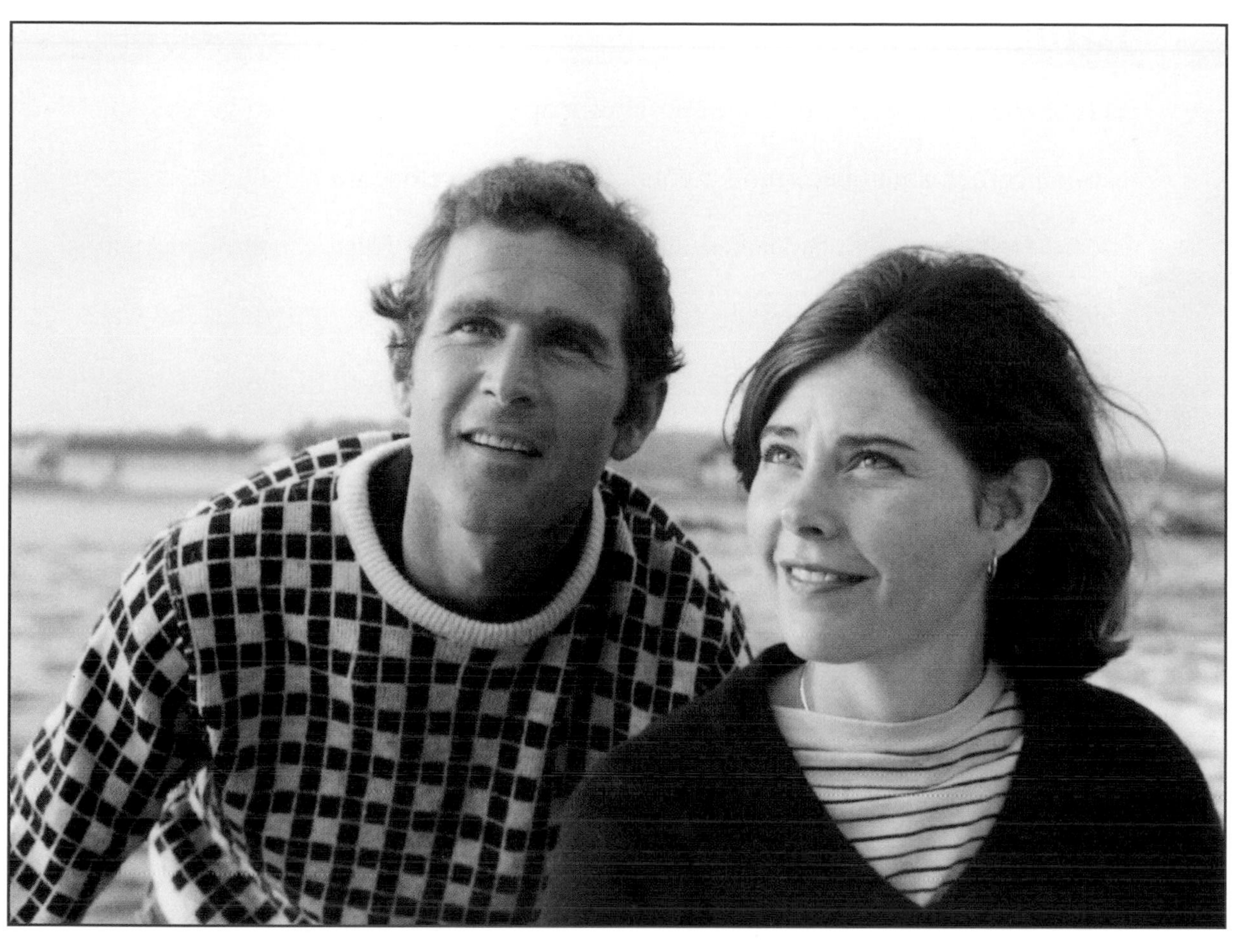

George and Laura Bush in 1977, the year they were married.

November 5, 1977, just three months after they met, George and Laura were married. Soon the Chinese slippers were gone and Laura began, ever so slowly, to become what George described as a "calming influence" on him.

Running for Office

Before she accepted George's proposal of marriage, Laura told George that she was concerned about becoming a politician's wife. For one thing, she was a registered Democrat. She had voted against George H. W. Bush for the Senate in 1970 and against Richard Nixon for president in 1972. More important, she was naturally shy. She valued her privacy and didn't want a spotlight shone on every detail of her private life. Nonetheless, she agreed to come along for the ride.

Laura quit her job and moved to Midland. Although George continued to develop Arbusto, the newlyweds spent much of their first year of marriage on the campaign trail. Bush was running for the local congressional seat against Democrat Kent Hance, a state senator and a professor of law in nearby Lubbock. Through the early months of the campaign both sides remained positive. In fact, when George learned some potentially damaging information about Hance, he refused to use it.

"George ran a nice-guy campaign," said Ernest Angelo, a former mayor of Midland. "I told him toward the end that you couldn't run a nice-guy campaign. He said, 'That's what Kent is doing too.' Well, sure enough, in the last ten days Kent Hance unloaded with everything but the kitchen sink."

As the campaign came to a close, Hance accused Bush of being a carpetbagger—a Yankee who wanted to interfere in Texas politics. He pointed out that

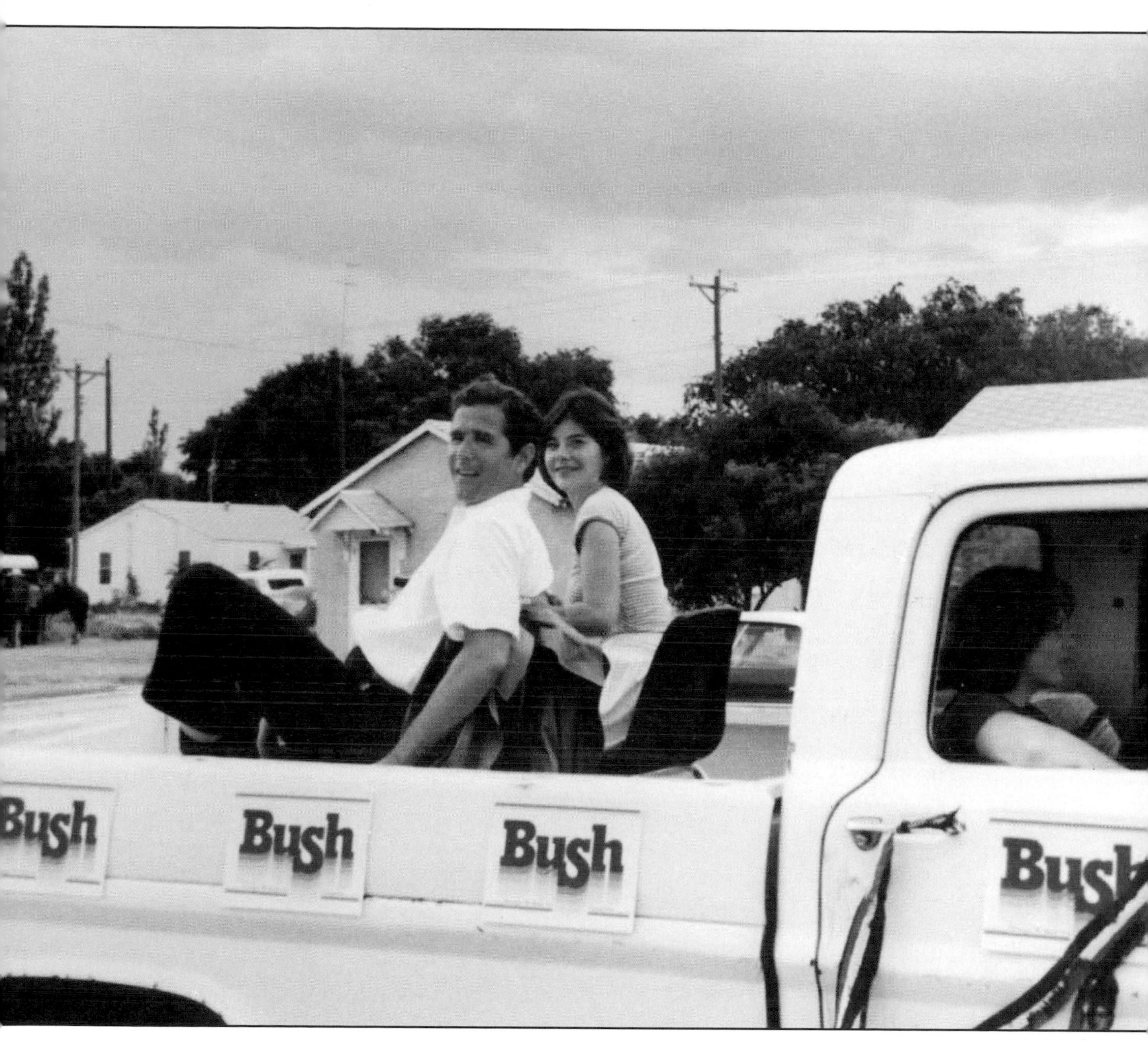

George and Laura Bush on the campaign trail in 1978. George lost his bid to win the seat in the U.S. House of Representatives representing a district that included Midland.

Bush was born in Connecticut and had gone to school at Andover, Yale, and Harvard. Hance completed his criticism by asserting that Bush had nothing to run on but "his daddy's coattails."

George and Laura Bush came closer together as they formed a united front against their opponent. Unfortunately Bush didn't have the time or the ammunition to recover from Hance's attacks, and he lost the election. The entire Bush family was devastated. Looking back at his defeat years later, George said, "Defeat humbles you. You work, you dream, you hope people see it your way, then suddenly it's over and they did not."

Crisis in Crude

The following years were a mixed blessing for George and Laura Bush. On the positive side, George's father was elected vice president of the United States in November 1980 as the running mate of Ronald Reagan. A year later, in November 1981, George and Laura's twin daughters were born. They were named Barbara and Jenna after their two grandmothers. As Laura later recalled, "George actually got up in the middle of the night and fed the babies with me and changed their diapers. One thing about having twins is you need a little bit of extra help."

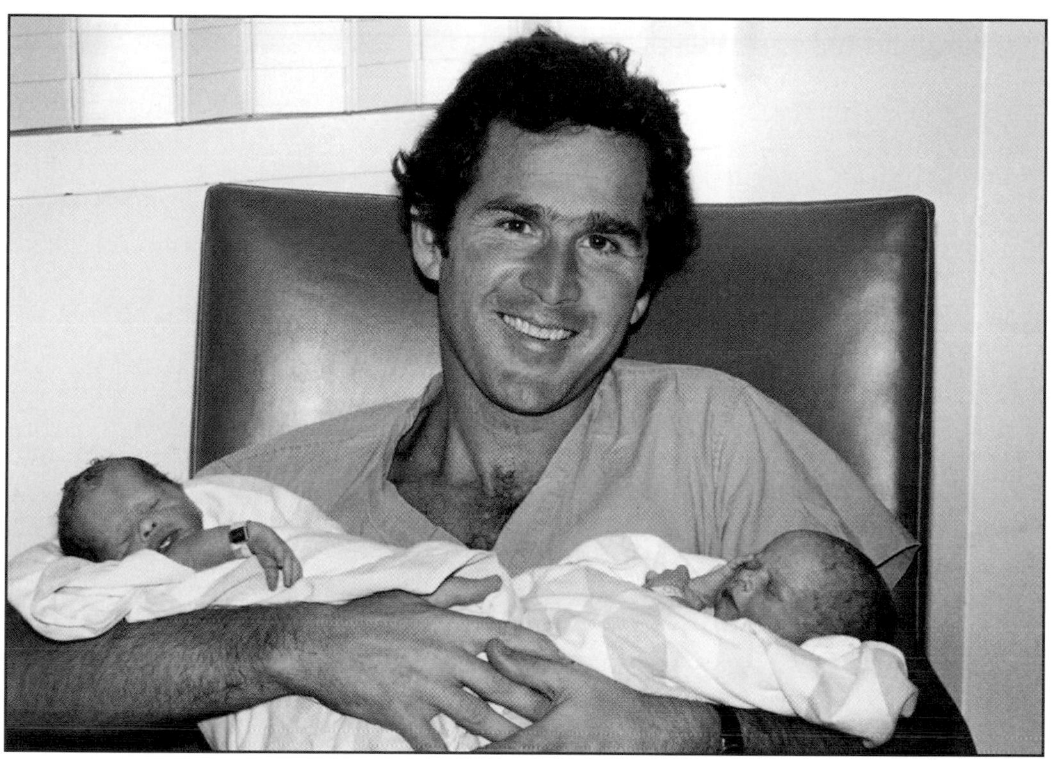

The happy father and his twin girls in November 1981. They were named Barbara and Jenna, after their two grandmothers.

On the other hand, George was less successful in business in the early 1980s. He found that his father's success made it easy to raise money from investors. In fact, he renamed Arbusto the Bush Exploration Company to take advantage of the name recognition. Still, without striking oil in a fair number of its exploratory wells, the business could not prosper. By 1984, the firm was in trouble. To avoid bankruptcy, Bush Exploration merged with Spectrum 7 Energy Corporation. However, oil prices were plummeting, and the new company, too, soon found itself teetering on the brink of bankruptcy.

In 1986 Spectrum 7 merged with the Harken Energy Corporation. Once again, George got a break because of his father's influence. Because he was the son of the vice president, George received a seat on Harken's board of directors, Harken stock worth more than $500,000, and a lucrative consulting contract worth $120,000 per year.

Saved and Sober

Through these ups and downs in his business, George's drinking continued, and it was beginning to affect his marriage. Laura was at her wit's end. Finally she gave George an ultimatum. "Laura basically went to him and told him he had to make a choice," said a friend. "'You've got these two beautiful girls and you've got me. You don't want to lose us over a bottle do you?'"

George clearly was facing a personal crisis, and he reached out for help. At the Bush family compound in Maine in the summer of 1985, he had a long talk with the Reverend Billy Graham, a famous Christian evangelist who had been a friend of presidents Eisenhower, Johnson, Nixon, Ford, and Reagan. Graham challenged George to think of himself as a child of God and to rely on God to fill the void in his soul.

"Are you right with God?" Graham asked.

"No, but I'd like to be," George replied.

Bush later said that Graham "planted a seed in my heart and I began to change." Still, he continued to drink heavily. His problem with alcohol finally reached a crisis a year later. On July 28, 1986, the day after his 40th birthday party, he woke up with a severe hangover. He looked in the mirror and saw a man in trouble. "I realized that alcohol was beginning to crowd out my energies," he later said, "and could crowd, eventually, my affections for other people. . . . When you're drinking, it can be an incredibly selfish act."

George vowed then and there that he would never take another drink. Since then, he said, he hasn't had a "drop of alcohol . . . not one drop." As his faith filled the void that George had once tried to fill with alcohol, friends and family members began to see George changing for the better. Laura and the girls noticed that he was becoming a better husband and father.

George's faith not only saved his personal life, but it set him on a new path that would have far-reaching consequences. "You know," George told a gathering of religious leaders in September 2002, "I had a drinking problem. Right now I

George Bush with his young family and his mother at a campaign rally for his father in 1984.

should be in a bar in Texas, not the Oval Office. There is only one reason that I am in the Oval Office and not in a bar. I found faith. I found God. I am here because of the power of prayer."

Poppy's Pit Bull

In 1987 President Ronald Reagan's second term was ending, and Vice President George H. W. Bush announced that he would campaign for the Republican nomination for president. The Bush family gathered to help "Poppy," as the Vice President had been known since childhood. George W. Bush moved to Washington and became an adviser to the campaign. He worked tirelessly to defend his father against opponents' charges and to end bickering in the Bush campaign. He was so effective that he earned a nickname of his own: "Poppy's Pit Bull."

George worked closely with Republican adviser Roger Ailes, who was the main architect of Republican campaign strategy against Democratic candidate Michael Dukakis. The plan was to paint the Massachusetts governor as a tax-and-spend liberal who was soft on crime. Ailes and his associates crafted a series of effective television advertisements that drilled these messages home. Democrats charged that Republicans were using smear tactics to win the election for George H. W. Bush.

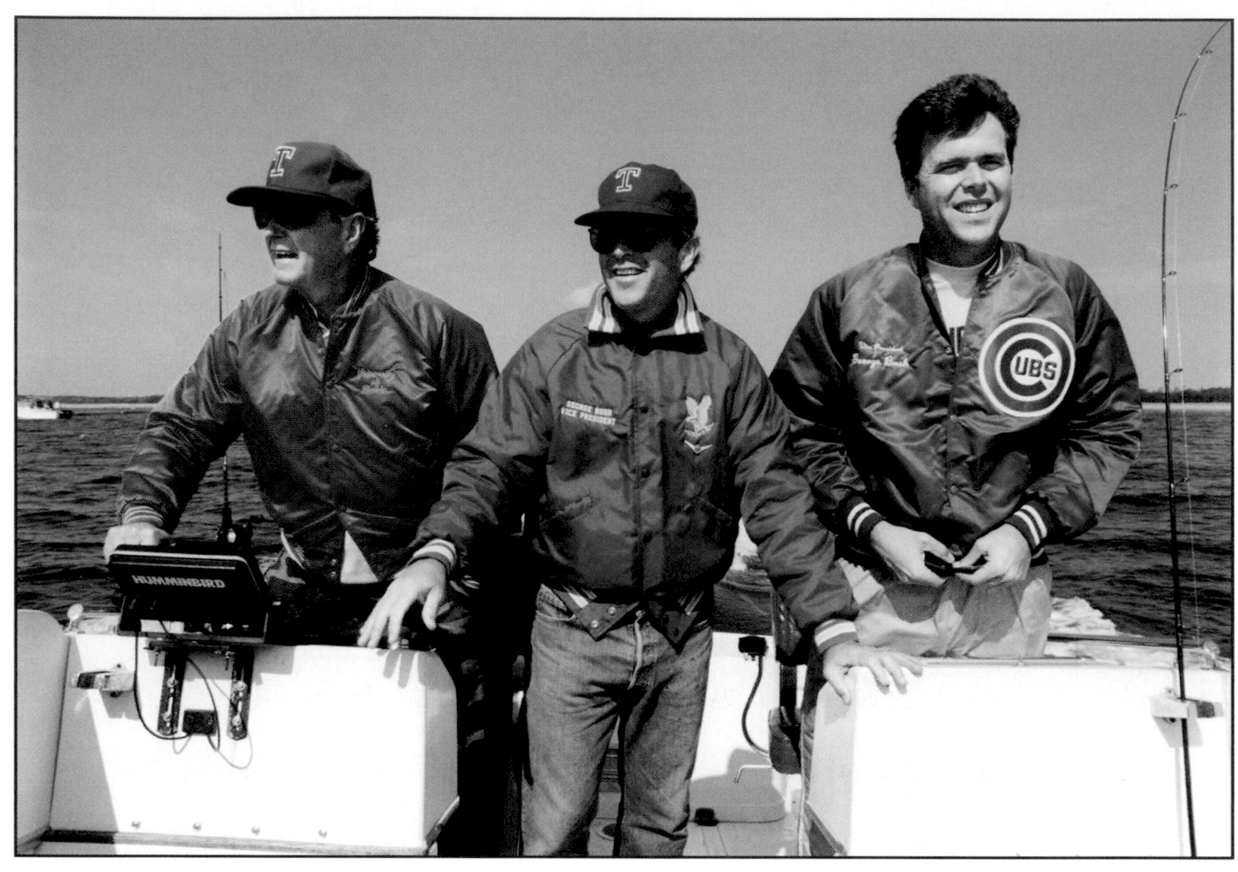

George and Jeb Bush with their father, President George H. W. Bush, in 1989. Both sons helped in their father's presidential campaign.

In November 1988, George H. W. Bush was elected president. Young George participated in early planning for his father's administration, making sure that Bush allies received positions of influence. Once the job was done, he and his family returned to Midland.

Chapter 4 Governor Bush

Baseball

Just before the 1988 presidential election, George W. Bush learned that the Texas Rangers baseball team was for sale. The Rangers played in Arlington, Texas, halfway between the state's second- and third-largest cities, Dallas and Fort Worth. The idea of owning a share of a baseball team was attractive to Bush, bringing together his love of baseball and his business skills. "He saw it as a great opportunity all around," said his father. "A chance to do something for Texas and a chance to be involved in baseball. It was everything he wanted."

On his return to Texas in early 1989, Bush helped assemble a group of investors to buy the team. As a prominent Texan and a son of the recently elected president, he received wide public attention. Late in April, the investment group bought the team for $85.4 million. Bush's share was $500,000, less than one percent of the total, but he was selected one of two managing directors with a reported salary of $200,000 a year. In June, Bush sold his Harken Energy stock, repaid the money he had borrowed to buy his share of the Rangers, and ended his career as an oilman. Now his job would be to manage the Rangers' local affairs and work with the community. The other managing director, Rusty Rose, took charge of the team's finances.

Bush described the Rangers in 1989 as "a team that had a 25-year losing record, sagging attendance, and an inferior ballpark." He became the most visible representative of the team in Arlington, attending most home games and announcing team plans. His biggest job was to persuade the city of Arlington to contribute funds toward building a new and improved stadium. With help from Bush and the Rangers, the city developed a plan to contribute $135 million toward the stadium by increasing the city sales tax, and in January 1991 voters approved it by a wide margin. Bush also arranged for passage of a bill in the Texas legislature that allowed the team to buy a valuable piece of Arlington real estate large enough to hold the stadium and new retail center. Before the end of that year, construction began.

The Ballpark at Arlington opened for the 1994 season, just in time to showcase the first Rangers team ever to qualify for the American League play-offs. Unfortunately, the Major League Players Association went on strike before the season ended, and the play-offs were canceled. Still, George Bush received

In 1989 George Bush became a managing director of the Texas Rangers, the major league baseball team in the Dallas–Fort Worth area.

widespread credit for his role in creating the new stadium and a more successful club. His accomplishments with the Rangers made him a widely known personality in the state—not as the son of a president, but as a success in his own right. "What's the boy ever done?" he asked a reporter at the time. "Well, now I can say I've done something." He pointed to the stadium. "Here it is."

Bush would soon resign as managing director to go into politics, but he continued to hold on to his financial interest in the club. Four years later, in 1998, the ownership group sold the Rangers for $250 million. Thanks to some bonus clauses in his contract, Bush's share of the profits was $14.9 million, a very handsome return on his investment.

The Persian Gulf War

Meanwhile, in Washington, the administration of the first George Bush faced a major crisis overseas. On August 2, 1990, the armies of Iraq invaded the neighboring nation of Kuwait, a small but oil-rich country on the Persian Gulf. Working with the United Nations, President Bush gained international condemnation of the takeover and of Iraq's leader, Saddam Hussein. When Saddam refused to remove Iraqi troops from Kuwait, the United States led a broad coalition of nations and assembled a huge military force in neighboring Saudi Arabia.

Iraq still refused to retreat, and the coalition began bombardment of Iraqi military positions in January 1991. After six weeks of bombing, they attacked on the ground, driving Iraqi troops out of Kuwait and into southern Iraq in just 100 hours of fighting. Some of the president's advisers urged him to send coalition forces all the way to Baghdad, the Iraqi capital, and overturn the dictatorial rule of Saddam Hussein, but the president refused. Instead, he chose to support economic sanctions on Iraq, which continued for twelve years.

At the end of the war, President Bush's popularity reached its high point, and it seemed almost certain that he would be re-elected for a second term in 1992. In the following months, however, his popularity began to slip. He broke a campaign promise made in 1988 by approving tax increases, causing an outcry from many fellow Republicans. In addition, the economy was sluggish and unemployment was increasing, and his opponents charged that the president did not appreciate the hardships people were suffering.

George W. Bush traveled frequently to Washington in 1992 to advise his father's campaign and help make difficult decisions. Democrats nominated Bill Clinton, a charming and politically moderate governor, to oppose Bush's re-election, and in November Clinton defeated the president. The loss was difficult for the whole Bush family, which never enjoyed losing. At the same time, the loss proved an opportunity for the president's sons. In 1994, both George W. and Jeb would run for governor in important states.

Governor Bush

Young George Bush first considered running for governor of Texas in 1990, but he had two strong reasons not to. Investors in the Texas Rangers gained a promise from him not to run for political office that year. In addition, his mother warned him that he would face strong disapproval from the voters if he ran while his father was only in his second year as president.

By 1994, George was free to run. His father had left the presidency in January 1993 after his defeat by Bill Clinton. In Texas, the Ballpark at Arlington had opened in the spring of 1994, and the team that year would be the best in the Rangers' history. George had a powerful reason to run as well. The present governor, Democrat Ann Richards, had made a national reputation by making fun of his father. In a speech at the Democratic convention in 1988, she had said, "Poor George. He can't help it. He was born with a silver foot in his mouth."

It turned out that 1994 was a banner year for Republicans. A group of young *conservative* Republican candidates won a majority in the U.S. House of Representatives for the first time in 42 years. These new members believed in reducing the size and scope of the federal government and in promoting tradi-

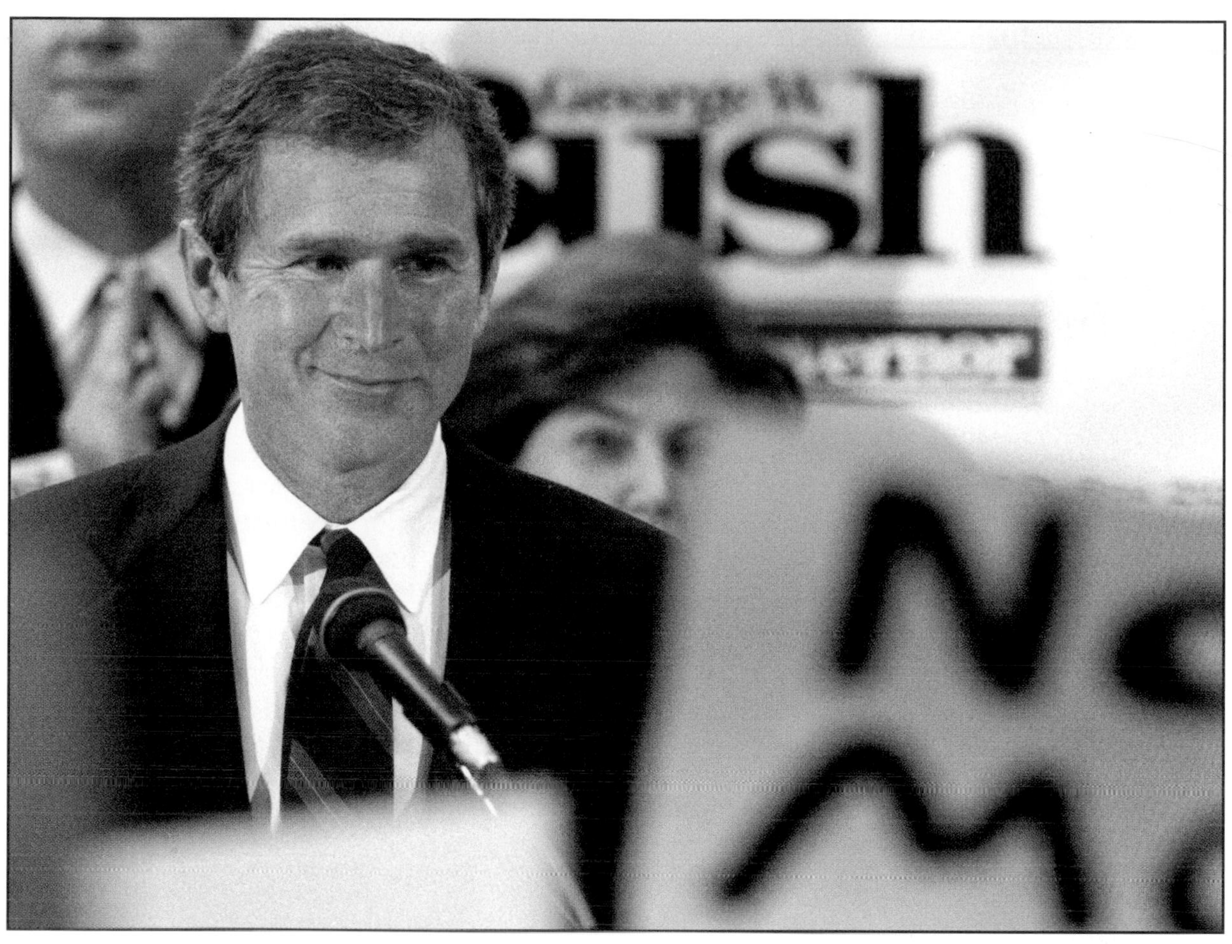

George Bush announces that he will run for governor of Texas in 1994.

tional values. In Texas, young George Bush ran a carefully disciplined campaign, concentrating on four simple issues and ignoring criticisms from the Democrats. He was elected with 54 percent of the vote. George's younger brother Jeb was running in the Florida governor's race that same day. Most family members had expected Jeb to win and George to lose, but George won and Jeb went down to defeat. For the first time, George W. Bush was the clear political winner in his family. It was his first electoral victory.

In his inaugural address on January 17, 1995, Bush praised the people of Texas and reaffirmed some of his key campaign promises. One of those promises was his pledge to return more decision-making power to Texas. "As governor, I will use every resource at my disposal to make the federal government in Washington heed this simple truth: Texans can run Texas," he said. "By trusting Texans, the state is more likely to focus on its principal responsibilities: good and safe streets, excellent schools, help for those who cannot help themselves, and respect for private property."

The new governor also pushed for reforms in the Texas state government. Working with the state legislature, he signed bills to reform welfare, education, and the juvenile justice system. He favored community action rather than government action to address problems such as drug abuse, broken families, and poverty. Still, he won friends among Democrats by supporting increased spending on public schools and bilingual education.

When it came time to run for re-election as governor in 1998, Bush returned to his conservative message and touted his accomplishments during his first term. He was re-elected with 68.2 percent of the vote.

Governor Bush urges Texas voters to support his billion-dollar tax cut in 1997.

The Lure of the Presidency

Even as Governor George W. Bush took the oath of office in January 1999, rumors swirled that he would run for president in 2000. In March 1999, he made the announcement. He faced a crowded field of Republicans eager to run. President Bill Clinton had been impeached by the House of Representatives during his second term for lying under oath about an inappropriate affair with a young White House intern. Even though Clinton had been acquitted in a trial before the Senate, his administration was tarnished by the scandal. Republicans believed they had a good chance to capture the White House in 2000.

Bush's leading Republican opponent was Senator John McCain, who fought in the Vietnam War and was held there as a prisoner of war for five years. McCain charged that Bush had used his father's influence to dodge military service in Vietnam and criticized Bush's conservative views. "I understand Governor Bush is now a reformer," McCain joked in February 2000. "If so, it's his first day on the job." Bush countered McCain by positioning himself as a pro-family Republican who would reduce taxes and bring an end to big government. The Bush campaign was also accused of running a smear campaign against McCain by allowing outside groups to run advertisements questioning McCain's sanity and his morals. By the end of March 2000, Bush had won enough primary elections to earn the Republican nomination. McCain later announced his support for Bush.

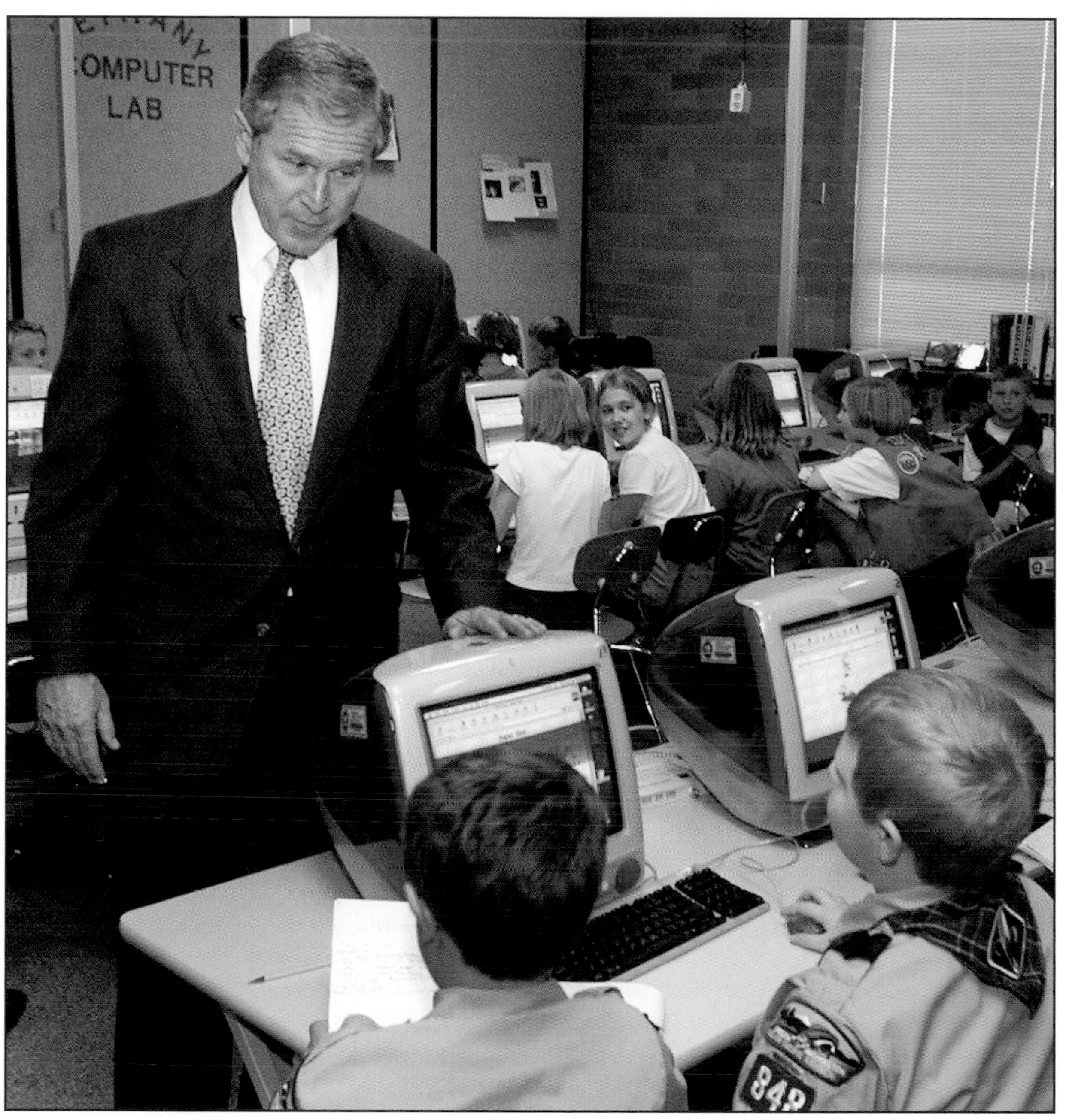

In 2000, as the Republican candidate for president, Bush visits a school computer lab in Oregon.

The Democrats nominated Clinton's vice president, Al Gore. Like Bush, Gore came from a prominent political family: both father and son had served in the U.S. Senate from Tennessee. Gore tried to distance himself from the Clinton scandals, and he pledged to continue policies that had led to strong economic growth and the first federal government surpluses in decades. Bush campaigned as a compassionate conservative and as a supporter of family values who could restore confidence in the presidency.

Election Night Chaos

By election day, it was clear that the vote would be extremely close. The nation was almost evenly divided between Bush and Gore. No one could have imagined how close the results actually were.

Late on election night, Al Gore was running slightly ahead of Bush in the popular vote. In the Electoral College, he appeared to have 266 of the 270 votes required to win the presidency. Bush had 246. In a few states, the vote was too close to make a prediction. The largest of these was Florida, which had 25 electoral votes. It became clear that whoever received the most popular votes in Florida would win the presidency.

Earlier that evening, television networks projected that Al Gore would win Florida. By 10 p.m., however, they said the state was "too close to call." At 2:17

The Electoral College

A president is not elected directly by individual voters. Voters are actually voting for *electors* from their state. The votes of these members of the Electoral College make the final decision. Each state has a number of electors equal to the number of representatives and senators it has in Congress. (The District of Columbia has three electoral votes even though it has no representatives or senators.) In most states, a candidate who wins the majority of popular votes wins all of that state's electors. Following the Constitution, the electors cast their votes in mid-December and the votes are officially counted in Congress on January 6. Of the 538 votes in the Electoral College, a candidate must receive a *majority* (one more than half, or 270) to gain election.

☆☆☆

a.m., they declared that Bush had won Florida and the presidency. Gore called Bush at 2:30 a.m. to concede defeat. An hour later, at 3:30 a.m., however, Bush's lead in the Florida ballot count dropped, and Gore called back to retract his concession. At 4:30 a.m., the networks again said the race was too close to call.

At the end of the counting, Bush led in Florida by a razor-thin margin of 1,784 votes, but there were many complaints of irregularities and calls for recounts in various counties. In one county, elderly Gore supporters claimed that a poorly designed "butterfly ballot" had misled them into voting for a third-party candidate instead of Gore. In some cities, African American voters insisted that they had been kept from voting at all. The Gore campaign argued that if these

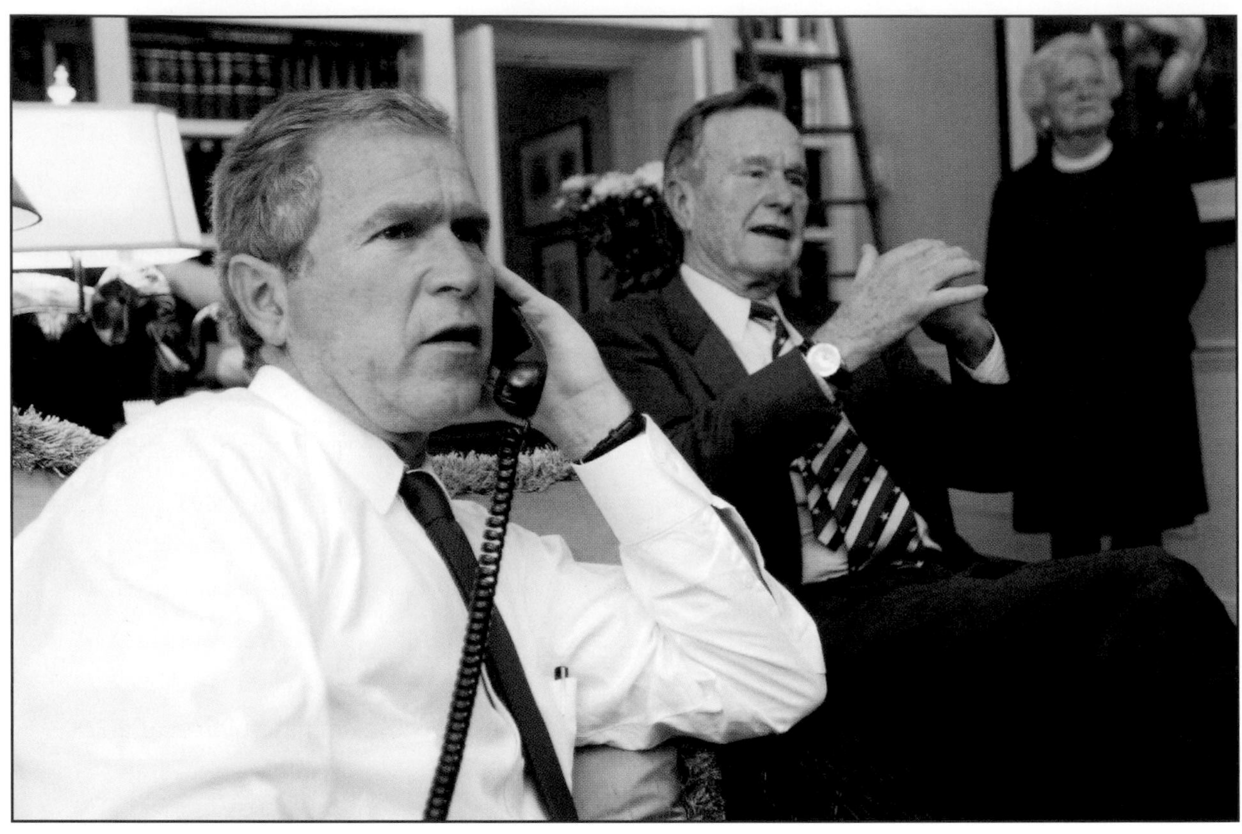

On election night 2000, Bush watches election results with his father and mother.

voters had been allowed to vote for the candidate of their choice, Gore would have won Florida and the presidency.

The disputes dragged on for weeks. Four Florida counties recounted their ballots. By November 26, Bush's lead was 537 votes. Secretary of State Katherine Harris (a member of Governor Jeb Bush's administration) awarded George Bush

Florida's Electoral College votes. These 25 votes gave Bush a total of 271, one more than he needed to win the presidency.

The legal challenges to the election results continued. On December 8, the Florida Supreme Court ordered 383 more votes to be added to Gore's total, dropping Bush's lead to 154 votes. The Gore campaign thought that victory was in sight.

However, on December 12, the United States Supreme Court, in a 5–4 decision, ruled that the manual recounts must end. The Court argued that because different Florida counties had different types of ballots, there could be no single standard for recounting, which meant that continued recounts would violate the equal protection clause of the United States Constitution.

With no more legal options left, Gore conceded defeat that evening, and the nation had a new president. Some later studies suggested that Bush would have won Florida and become president even if the recounts had been continued. Yet Gore continued to lead in the popular vote by more than 500,000, and many who supported him continued to believe that the outcome of the election was unfair.

Uniting a Nation

On the evening of December 13, 2000, President-elect Bush addressed the nation and stressed that "Americans share hopes and goals and values far more important than any political disagreements. Republicans want the best for our nation, and so do Democrats. Our votes may differ, but not our hopes." Vice President Gore agreed, adding, "this belatedly broken impasse can point us all to a new common ground, for its very closeness can serve to remind us that we are one people with a shared history and a shared destiny."

Chapter 5

Mr. President

Compassionate Conservatism

On January 20, 2001, George W. Bush took the oath of office to become the 43rd president of the United States. In his inaugural address he discussed the themes of "civility, courage, compassion, and character."

When Bush took office, the U.S. economy was at the top of a long economic boom. Rising stock market prices, especially for rapidly growing computer and electronics companies, had fueled a spectacular economic expansion. Individuals and businesses were not the only ones to benefit. For the first time in decades, the federal government was projecting large budget surpluses. Because people and businesses were earning more, they were paying more taxes, and the government was bringing in more money than it was spending.

January 2001: George W. Bush is sworn in as president.

The budget surplus was one reason for Bush to propose a large tax cut soon after his inauguration. He said that the government should return some of this "extra" money to taxpayers rather than finding new ways to spend it. Bush and his economic advisers also believed that a tax cut could help stimulate the economy. As the great stock market boom ended and the economy slowed down, the president emphasized that tax cuts could help get the economy moving again.

The Republican-controlled Congress passed Bush's program of federal income tax reductions in May 2001, reducing them by $1.35 trillion over ten years. Democrats criticized the cuts, arguing that the government's income was likely to decline as the boom came to an end. They also pointed out that the tax cut plan saved huge amounts for the very richest Americans, while savings for poor and middle-class Americans were much smaller.

In May 2001, the president unveiled an energy strategy that had been written by an energy task force chaired by Vice President Dick Cheney. One of its goals was reducing American dependence on oil from overseas, and it proposed drilling for oil in the Arctic National Wildlife Refuge in Alaska. Some environmentalists argued that Arctic regions were easily damaged and that exploration would endanger many rare plants and animals. Opponents of the new oil exploration stalled the energy plan in Congress.

The energy strategy came under increasing criticism when Vice President Cheney refused to reveal the names of outside advisers who helped write the Bush energy policy. Critics suggested that the proposals came from executives of energy companies and that no environmentalists or conservationists had been consulted.

Another initiative proposed by the president in his first months was a 4-year, $38-billion bill to reform Medicare, the program that provides basic medical insurance for retired and disabled people. The proposed reform included the first provision of a benefit for prescription drugs. The proposal received widespread support from senior citizens, many of whom were paying hundreds of dollars a month for medications prescribed by their doctors. The seniors were disappointed a few months later, however. After the September 11 attacks on New York and Washington, D.C., Congress tabled Medicare reform while the country dealt with a national emergency.

Medicare reform was finally introduced again in 2003. After a difficult and divisive debate, Congress passed a reform that was expected to cost $400 billion over ten years. When President Bush signed the bill into law on December 8, 2003, he said, "These reforms are the act of a vibrant and compassionate government. We show our concern for the dignity of our seniors by giving them quality

Vice President Dick Cheney

Vice President Richard Cheney.

George Bush had chosen Richard Cheney to be his running mate for vice president. Cheney, five years older than the president, had served in a variety of government posts. He was named White House chief of staff by President Gerald Ford in 1976. In 1978 he was elected to the first of five terms in the U.S. House of Representatives from his home state of Wyoming. From 1989 to 1993, under the first President Bush, Cheney was secretary of defense, serving during the first Persian Gulf War. In the 1990s Cheney became chief executive officer of Halliburton, a large and powerful company offering industrial and military services. It received much of its income from large contracts with the U.S. government.

Bush and Cheney had much in common. They were both Westerners who had been involved with the oil industry in the region. They had gained their influence through the conservative wing of the Republican party and both favored aggressive energy and defense policies. In 2001 they began to work together to combat terrorism and develop a national energy policy.

health care." Advocates for the elderly were not so hopeful. They pointed out that full benefits would not be paid until 2006 and that the program before then was so complicated that many seniors would never enroll. On the other side of the issue, conservatives believed the reform was too generous, offering benefits to millions of retirees who could afford to pay for their own medications.

A World Transformed

The events of September 11, 2001, changed the direction of George Bush's presidency. After the terrorist attacks on the World Trade Center in New York and the Pentagon in Washington, D.C., the president mobilized the country for a war against terrorism. The administration's domestic proposals received far less attention. When he began campaigning for a second term in 2004, President Bush said, "The world changed on September the 11th, and since that day, we have changed the world."

An immediate effect of the attacks was that Americans lined up behind the president in the country's hour of danger. The divisions and disputes of the 2000 election were forgotten, and all of America seemed to be rooting for Bush. One *public opinion poll* (a survey of a representative sample of people reached by phone or in person to determine the views of a much larger group) showed that 86 percent of the American people supported him.

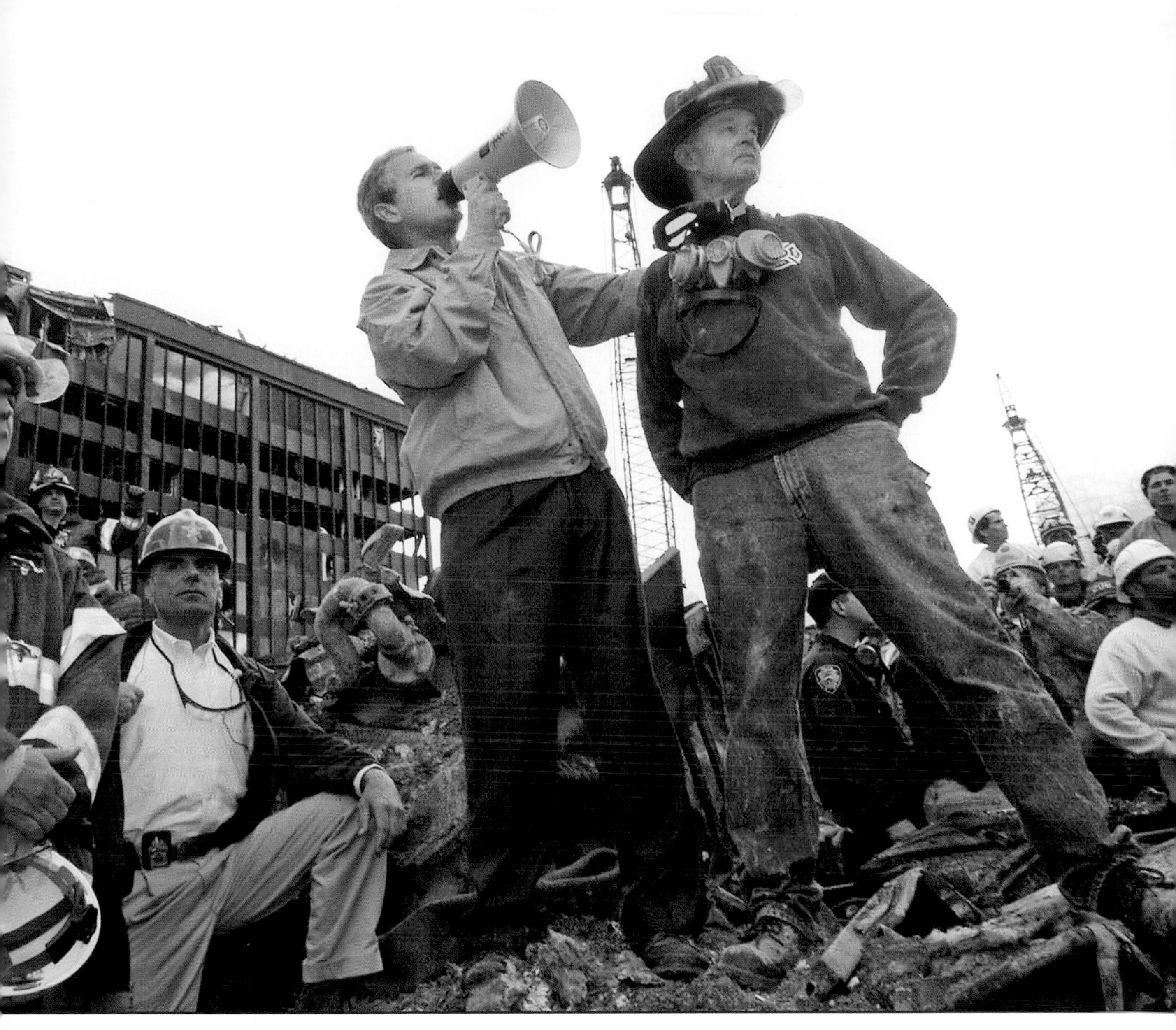

September 14, 2001: Three days after the terrorist attacks, President Bush uses a bullhorn to address rescue workers at the World Trade Center site in New York City.

Even with wide support, the administration had complicated issues to face. Congressional leaders urged the formation of a new federal department to help prevent further terrorist attacks. President Bush resisted these calls at first, but he soon changed his mind. In 2002 he worked with Congress to create the new Department of Homeland Security made up largely of agencies that had been parts of other departments.

In October 2001, before the new Homeland Security Department could be established, Bush proposed and Congress passed the Patriot Act, a bill that addressed a wide range of security concerns. Among its goals was encouraging greater sharing of information about suspected terrorists between U.S. intelligence services; easing restrictions on intelligence investigators; and providing better security at national borders. Most Americans favored these actions to reduce the threat of terrorist attacks. However, civil liberties organizations warned that some provisions of the Patriot Act could threaten individual freedoms by allowing security agents to collect personal information about individuals without prior approval by a court.

Action Overseas

It quickly became clear that the September 11 attacks on New York and Washington were planned and carried out by al-Qaeda, an international terrorist network based in Afghanistan and directed by Osama bin Laden, a known terrorist leader. President Bush quickly gathered a broad coalition of countries that were united in their desire to attack al-Qaeda's bases in Afghanistan and to capture Osama bin Laden.

On September 20, 2001, the United States demanded that the fundamentalist Muslim rulers of Afghanistan, known as the Taliban, turn over bin Laden to American authorities. When this request was denied, the United States launched a military operation dubbed Operation Enduring Freedom. Its aims were first to disrupt al-Qaeda operations in the country and second to remove the Taliban from power. A combined air and ground offensive conducted by American, British, and anti-Taliban Afghan forces routed the Taliban, and on November 13 they captured the Afghan capital of Kabul. Coalition forces then launched raids into the rugged mountains along the Afghan-Pakistani border, seeking al-Qaeda camps and leaders. Many camps were discovered and some terrorist leaders were captured, but Osama bin Laden managed to escape.

In the months after the September 11 attacks, President Bush began to formulate a new policy, which became known as the Bush Doctrine. He stated it most clearly in a commencement address at the U.S. Military Academy in June 2002. The doctrine states that to prevent a terrorist attack the United States will take *preemptive action*—attack a terrorist group or a rogue state without warning

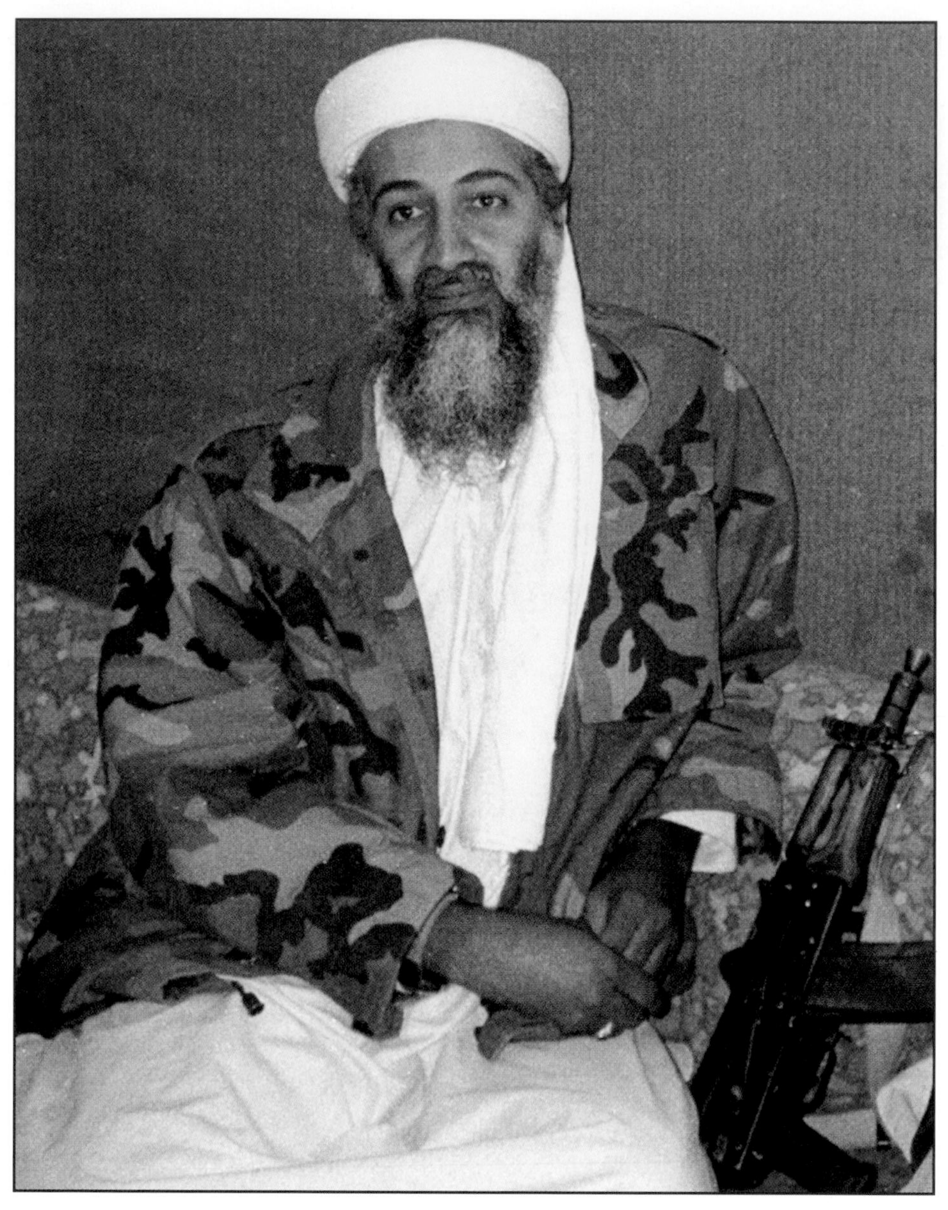

Osama bin Laden, the leader of al-Qaeda, the terrorist network that planned and carried out the attacks on the United States on September 11, 2001.

and without consulting its allies or international organizations. The doctrine also provides that U.S. attacks would make no distinction between terrorists and those who harbored and protected them. In Afghanistan, coalition forces attacked both al-Qaeda (the terrorists) and the Taliban (the government that protected the terrorist group). The Bush Doctrine drew heavy criticism around the world. Many U.S. friends and enemies alike suggested that the Bush Doctrine sounded like a bully's threats and could be a danger to world peace.

Soon after occupying the Afghan capital of Kabul, the United States began organizing a provisional Afghan government directed by Hamid Karzai, who was sworn in on December 22, 2001. Since much of the country beyond Kabul remained in the control of local warlords, American troops remained in Afghanistan to expand the area controlled by the government, eliminate pockets of pro-Taliban resistance, and disrupt al-Qaeda operations. Many Taliban and al-Qaeda fighters who were captured during skirmishes there were transported to the U.S. base at Guantánamo Bay, Cuba, where they were held by U.S. authorities for interrogation, without being charged with crimes or tried.

In January 2004, Afghan tribal leaders signed a constitution guaranteeing basic freedoms denied by the Taliban, and in October 2004 President Karzai was elected in a generally free presidential election. Tribal warlords continued to have wide influence in the Karzai government, but the United States continued to hope that the country would gradually develop truly democratic institutions.

The Widening War on Terror

Almost immediately after September 11, some in the Bush administration wanted to extend the war on terror to Iraq. It had been more than ten years since the United Nations coalition led by the first President Bush had driven Iraqi troops out of Kuwait. Since then, the brutal dictator Saddam Hussein remained in power. His economic and military activities had been restrained by *sanctions*, restrictions on trade with other countries administered by the United Nations. In addition, Iraq had received regular visits from UN inspectors who searched for nuclear, chemical, and biological weapons. Still, hard-liners in the Bush administration argued that Saddam was as much a danger to the United States and the rest of the world as al-Qaeda.

In his first State of the Union address, in January 2002, President Bush praised the success of the Afghan war, but he warned that other dangers were lurking. "What we have found in Afghanistan confirms that, far from ending there, our war against terror is only beginning," he said. Bush went on to mention the nations of Iraq, North Korea, and Iran, which he said "constitute an axis of evil, arming to threaten the peace of the world."

The president saw Iraq as the most immediate threat. "All [Saddam's] terrible features became much more threatening," Bush later recalled. "Keeping Saddam in a box [of UN sanctions] looked less and less feasible to me." He wanted to remove Saddam from power, and he was beginning to formulate a twofold case for going to war.

First, he argued that Saddam was linked to al-Qaeda. Although the Bush administration never claimed that Iraq was involved in the September 11 attacks, it argued that over the course of a decade Iraq had developed a cooperative relationship with al-Qaeda. They suggested that Iraq had provided al-Qaeda with money, weapons, and training to attack Westerners around the world. The White House asserted that Osama bin Laden himself met with officers of Iraq's secret police during the 1990s, and that al-Qaeda began to operate terrorist camps in Iraq even before the September 11 attacks. These assertions were widely disputed by experts on terrorism, including some who had served in the Bush administration, but spokesmen continued to suggest that there was a real and significant tie between Iraq and al-Qaeda.

The second reason to overthrow Saddam Hussein was the belief that the Iraqi government possessed weapons of mass destruction, including chemical, biological, and nuclear weapons that could be used against Iraq's neighbors or even against the United States. At first, the administration favored reestablishing

UN arms inspections in Iraq, but when the work proved to be slow and the conclusions unclear, it soon lost patience and began advocating an invasion.

The Bush administration went to the United Nations Security Council to gain support of other world leaders to attack Iraq and overthrow Saddam Hussein. Secretary of State Colin Powell made a detailed presentation of U.S.

Secretary of State Colin Powell addresses the United Nations Security Council in February 2003, urging other nations to support an invasion of Iraq.

assertions and suspicions. Despite this strong campaign, the Bush administration was unable to persuade most of its closest allies, including France and Germany, to support military action to remove Saddam from power. Some ordinary citizens in the United States and in many countries around the world took to the streets in massive demonstrations against the Bush administration's drumbeat for war in Iraq.

Striking Saddam

By April 2002, it had become clear that Bush was leaning ever closer to attacking Iraq using U.S. troops. "Obviously I want to make sure we do this right and quickly," Bush said privately to Tommy Franks, head of U.S. Central Command. The plan was for soldiers to race through vast stretches of desert, reach Baghdad, and quickly topple Saddam Hussein's regime. Bush's foreign policy team expected that the Americans would be greeted as heroes and liberators and that democracy would quickly take root.

In the end several dozen smaller countries supported the Bush administration by sending military forces to Iraq or providing logistical support, but only two—Great Britain and Australia—sent a sizable number of troops. For the United States, Bush believed, the war was a matter of self-defense, and time was of the essence.

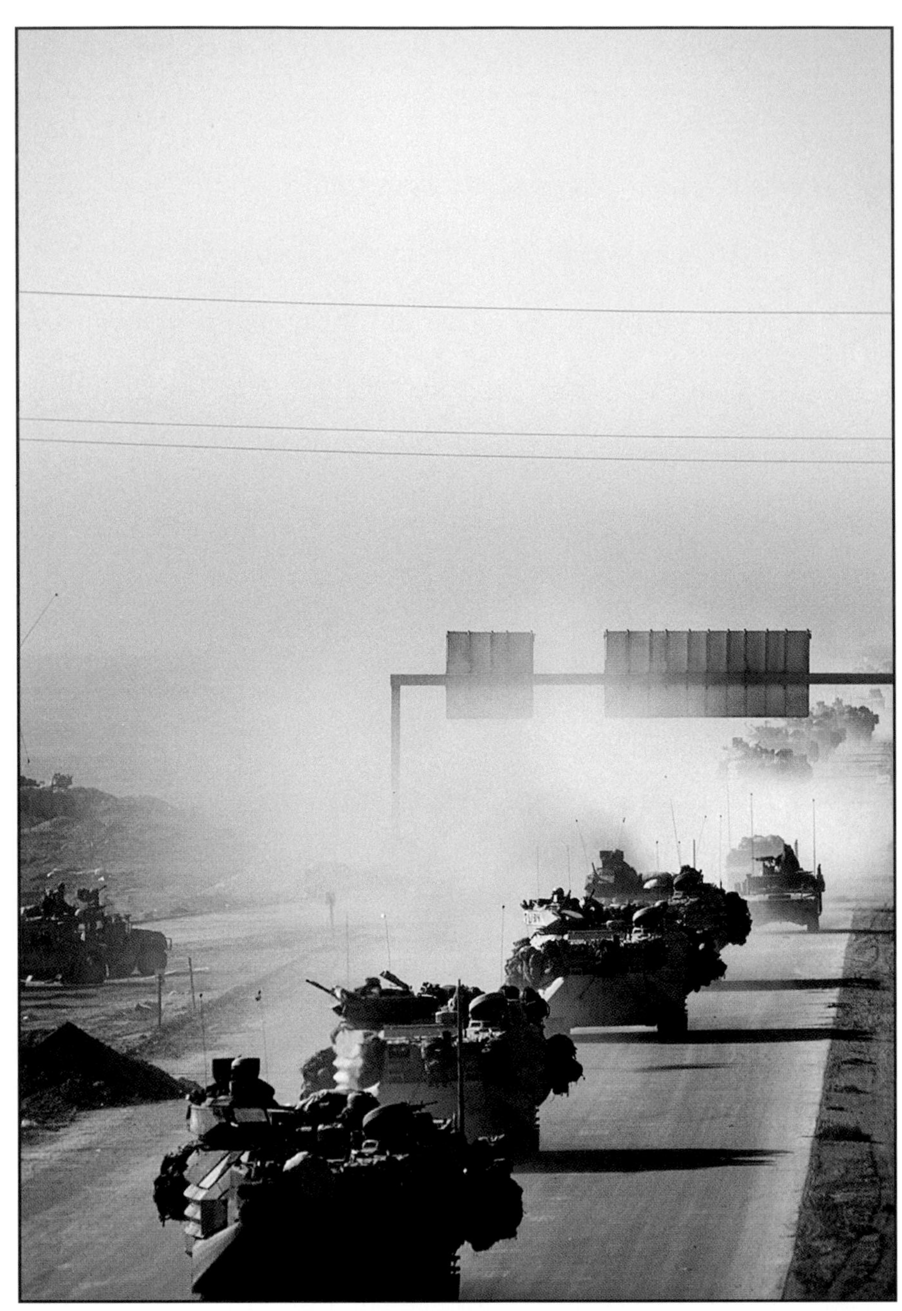

United States Marines on the road to Baghdad in April 2003.

Saddam was given new opportunities to prove that he had destroyed all of his country's weapons of mass destruction, but war preparations continued. By March 2003, nearly 300,000 American troops had arrived in the Persian Gulf region. On March 20, 2003, after declaring that Saddam had violated United Nations resolutions calling on him to disarm, the coalition began a massive air and ground assault on Iraq called Operation Iraqi Freedom.

Iraqis topple a statue of deposed dictator Saddam Hussein.

Military strategists described the campaign as "shock and awe" because of the speed with which the troops moved and the firepower that was on display. By April 12, American forces had captured the capital city of Baghdad. Only three weeks after the war began, the regime of Saddam Hussein was no more. It was one of the quickest and most successful military campaigns in modern history. Many of Saddam's finest troops simply melted away without putting up serious resistance. Only later did it become clear that many of these troops disappeared to rearm, returning later to resist the coalition forces.

Chapter 6

Fighting for a Second Term

Mission Accomplished?

On May 1, 2003, President Bush landed in a U.S. Navy fighter plane on the deck of the aircraft carrier *Abraham Lincoln*. On the carrier's deck, standing in front of a large banner saying "Mission Accomplished," the president announced to the nation that "major combat operations in Iraq have ended." He said there was still "difficult work to do" in rebuilding Iraq and pledged that forces there would "track down the leaders of the old regime." The United States offered a reward of $25 million for information leading to the arrest of Saddam Hussein. In July, Saddam's two sons, both important aides to their father, were killed by American troops, but Saddam continued to evade capture.

Finally, on December 13, 2003, Saddam was captured by American soldiers near his hometown of Tikrit hiding in an underground tunnel. President Bush was overjoyed at the news. "For the vast majority of Iraqi citizens who wish to live as free men and women," he said, "this event brings further assurance that the torture chambers and the secret police are gone forever." U.S. soldiers sent Saddam's handgun to the president, who had it mounted on a plaque and hung in his private study.

The Price of Freedom

In the year after the president's speech on the *Abraham Lincoln*, several terrorist groups continued to attack U.S. and coalition forces. More Americans were killed in the year after the president's speech than in the original invasion. Thousands of Iraqi civilians had also been killed in continuing violence.

Attacks were particularly fierce in the Sunni Muslim region of central Iraq, Saddam Hussein's home area. These fighters were well supplied, apparently with military supplies hidden before and after the U.S. invasion. At the same time, Shia Muslims, long oppressed by Saddam Hussein, mounted attacks against the United States and its allies. Shia Muslims made up a majority in Iraq and were hoping to gain political control of the country. Both Sunni and Shia fighters used terrorist tactics, including suicide bombings and use of homemade explosives. In addition, the fighting attracted al-Qaeda fighters and other Muslim terrorists who saw an opportunity to strike a blow against the United States.

Terrorist attacks on Iraq's oil fields and pipelines continued in 2004, more than a year after U.S. forces captured Baghdad.

The U.S. occupation authorities worked to restore stability in Iraq by providing reliable water and electricity supplies and establishing law and order. In the year after the capture of Baghdad, several thousand schools and hundreds of health clinics were built or restored. Hundreds of towns received aid for reconstruction, and more than 5 million children were vaccinated. Terrorists continued their attacks, however. Hundreds of Iraqis who accepted jobs with the U.S.-supported government were killed in ambushes and suicide bombings. Foreign workers were kidnapped and held for ransom or killed. Oil pipelines were attacked and damaged. Many international groups, including United Nations agencies, the International Red Cross, and CARE International, withdrew from the country because of continuing dangers to their workers.

The U.S.-led coalition forces also worked to hasten the day when Iraqis could take over their government. In June 2004, the occupation government returned sovereignty to a provisional Iraqi government. Nationwide elections were planned for January 2005. Still, it appeared that U.S. forces would remain in Iraq for years to come.

The Battle at Home

During 2004, President Bush faced a series of difficult issues as he prepared to run for a second term in November. As the fighting continued in Iraq and U.S. casualties increased, the president's critics questioned his decision to invade Iraq in the first place. Governor Howard Dean of Vermont, who was running for the Democratic presidential nomination, expressed doubts that the invasion of Iraq advanced the war on terror. He argued that Saddam Hussein's government had refused to cooperate with al-Qaeda in the 1990s. As the presidential campaign progressed, other Democratic candidates took up this argument, claiming that Iraq was "a detour" in the fight against terrorism.

At the same time, questions had arisen about the president's claim that Iraq had weapons of mass destruction. After a year of U.S. occupation, no major stockpiles of such weapons had been found. In fact, it appeared that Iraq's nuclear weapons program had been ended years earlier. President Bush was forced to concede that the prewar intelligence pointing to vast stockpiles of weapons of mass destruction had been faulty. Republicans insisted that Iraq had intended to make such weapons and had the materials to make them in the future.

In the meantime, the government commission studying the September 11 attacks held public hearings and released its written report. The commission, made up of respected members of both parties, harshly criticized the performance of U.S. intelligence organizations. It argued that the 9/11 attacks might have been prevented if the Central Intelligence Agency, the FBI, and other intelligence groups had shared information on terrorism. The commission found fault with both the Bush and Clinton administrations and urged major changes in intelligence gathering.

Bush vs. Kerry

In July 2004, the Democratic party nominated Massachusetts senator John Kerry for president. Kerry, who was a veteran of combat in Vietnam and later a leader of Vietnam Veterans Against the War, emphasized his military service and contrasted it to Bush's "safe" enlistment in the Texas National Guard. Kerry also kept up the criticism against the war in Iraq and attacked Republican policies on the economy and health care.

In September, the Republicans met in New York City, a few miles from the World Trade Center site, to nominate George W. Bush for a second term. "I'm asking for four more years to make our country safer, to make the economy stronger, to make our future better and brighter for every single citizen," Bush said. "From creating jobs to improving schools to fighting terror to protecting our homeland, we have made progress—and there is more to do."

The war in Iraq and the war on terrorism dominated the debate between the candidates. Senator Kerry argued that the war on terrorism must be conducted jointly with other nations and with the support of the United Nations. President Bush contended that the United States should act alone if necessary against threats to its national security. Kerry also argued that the invasion of Iraq had been a mistake that had given encouragement to terrorists and made the United States less safe. It appeared that voters were equally divided between the two

Senator John Kerry, the Democratic candidate for president, campaigns against President Bush in 2004.

candidates. Public opinion polls showed that a majority were critical of President Bush on Iraq. At the same time, a majority believed he would be a stronger defender of U.S. interests in the world.

Democrats also campaigned on economic issues. They charged that Bush's tax cuts had provided little relief to the middle class and had led to ever-increasing federal deficits. President Bush concentrated his criticism on John Kerry personally, suggesting again and again that Kerry "flip-flopped" on important issues and could not be trusted in a prolonged struggle against terrorism.

High interest in the campaign resulted in a large increase in voter registrations and in a huge turnout at the polls. Both parties expressed fears that the election might be a repeat of 2000, in which voters were so equally divided that the election was a source of controversy and bitterness.

Four More Years

On November 2, 2004, a larger percentage of registered voters went to the polls than in any election since 1968. As in 2000, state-by-state results were close. By the following morning, however, it was clear that President Bush had won a second term in office. In the popular vote, Bush led by nearly 3.5 million, receiving 51 percent of the vote to Kerry's 48 percent. In the Electoral College, Bush had 286 votes, 16 more than a majority, to Kerry's 252. Republicans also added to their slim majorities in the House of Representatives and the Senate.

Exit polls revealed that a majority of Americans supported President Bush because they felt he would keep them safer at home, even though they were unhappy with the conduct of the war in Iraq. He also received strong support from Americans who identified themselves as practicing Christians. These voters believed that Bush stood with them on such family issues as limiting access to abortion and opposing gay marriage. Experts said that their votes helped tip the balance for Bush in the key states of Ohio and Florida.

President Bush and Vice President Cheney, who were elected to a second term in November 2004.

In his acceptance speech on November 3, Bush said, "America has spoken, and I'm humbled by the trust and the confidence of my fellow citizens." He vowed to work with congressional Democrats to pass important legislation. Senator Kerry pledged to continue pressing for the Democratic agenda from his seat in the Senate.

As George W. Bush began his second term, he still faced a variety of challenges. The situation in Iraq remained dangerous even though the election of a new Iraqi government was approaching. Other world trouble spots included Iran and North Korea, which both had nuclear weapons and were members of Bush's "axis of evil."

At home, he faced a divided public. His strongest supporters urged him to use his second term to pursue longtime conservative goals, while the 48 percent who voted for his opponent in 2004 urged him to take steps to bring the country together. One observer wrote, "The leader who could begin to mend the rifts in this country would leave a significant legacy behind for history to applaud and admire. All it would require is courage and confidence."

PRESIDENTIAL

Fast Facts

George W. Bush

Birth:	July 6, 1946
Birthplace:	New Haven, Connecticut
Parents:	George H. W. Bush and Barbara Pierce Bush
Brothers & Sisters:	Pauline (Robin) (1949–1953) John (Jeb) (1953–) Neil (1955–) Marvin (1956–) Dorothy (1959–)
Education:	Yale University, B.A. 1968 Harvard Business School, M.B.A. 1975
Occupation:	Businessman
Marriage:	To Laura Welch, November 5, 1977
Children:	(*see* First Lady Fast Facts at right)
Political Party:	Republican
Public Offices:	1995–2001 Governor of Texas 2001– 43rd President of the United States
His Vice President:	Richard B. Cheney
Major Actions as President:	2001 Signed a 10-year, $1.35 trillion income tax cut 2001 Defeated Taliban-led regime in Afghanistan 2003 Defeated regime of Saddam Hussein in Iraq 2005 Congratulated Iraq on its first free elections

FIRST LADY

Fast Facts Laura Welch Bush

Birth:	November 4, 1946
Birthplace:	Midland, Texas
Parents:	Harold Welch and Jenna Welch
Brothers & Sisters:	None
Education:	Southern Methodist University, B.A. 1968 University of Texas at Austin, M.L.S. 1973
Marriage:	To George W. Bush, November 5, 1977
Children:	Jenna (1981–) Barbara (1981–)

Timeline

1946

George W. Bush born to George H. W. and Barbara Pierce Bush in New Haven, Connecticut, July 6.

1948

Family moves to Odessa, Texas.

1950

Family moves to Midland, Texas.

1953

Robin Bush, George's 3-year-old sister, dies.

1959

Family moves to Houston, Texas.

1977

Starts oil exploration firm Arbusto (later Bush Exploration); marries Laura Welch, November 5.

1978

Loses election for seat in U.S. House of Representatives.

1981

Twin daughters Jenna and Barbara born, November 25.

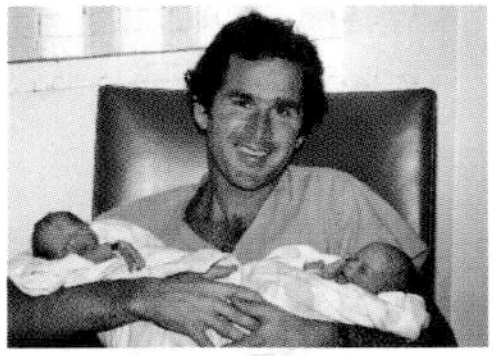

1984

Bush Exploration merges with Spectrum 7.

1985

Bush experiences reawakening of his Christian faith.

1998

Sells his share in Texas Rangers; elected to second term as Texas governor.

1999

Announces campaign for Republican presidential nomination in 2000.

2000

Wins nomination, defeats Democrat Al Gore in disputed national election.

2001

Inaugurated, January 20; signs landmark tax reduction bill, June.

2001

After September 11 attacks on New York City and Washington, Bush declares war on terrorism; U.S. leads attack on Afghanistan.

1961

Bush enrolls at Phillips Academy in Andover, Massachusetts.

1964

Enrolls at Yale University in New Haven, Connecticut.

1968

Graduates from Yale; joins the Texas Air National Guard.

1973

Enrolls at Harvard Business School in Cambridge, Massachusetts.

1975

Graduates from Harvard Business School; moves to Midland, Texas.

1986

Resolves to stop drinking alcohol; Spectrum 7 merges with Harken Energy.

1988

Bush serves as adviser in father's presidential campaign; George H. W. Bush elected president.

1989

George W. Bush purchases stake in the Texas Rangers baseball team, becomes a managing director.

1992

George H. W. Bush defeated for re-election by Democrat Bill Clinton.

1994

George W. Bush elected governor of Texas, defeating Governor Ann Richards.

2003

U.S. and coalition partners attack Iraq, overthrow government of Saddam Hussein.

2004

Bush wins second term, defeating Democrat John Kerry in close national election.

2005

Inaugurated, January 20.

Glossary

assassination: the murder of a head of state or other political leader

Communist: a person who favors a political system in which the state owns and manages all property and business

conservative: a person who believes in reducing the size and scope of government and in promoting traditional values

draft: a system in which the government can call up able-bodied young men for military service

elector: as outlined in the U.S. Constitution, a person elected by voters in a state to cast a vote for U.S. president and vice president in the Electoral College, the body that formally elects these officers

majority: in an election, one more than half of the votes; in a legislature, the party that holds a majority of the seats

preemptive action: a military strike carried out without warning to prevent a grave danger such as a terrorist attack

public opinion poll: a survey of a representative sample of people reached by phone or in person that can indicate the views of a much larger group

sanctions: restrictions imposed by an international organization or a group of nations on a state that has broken international law or agreements; the United Nations imposed economic sanctions on Iraq

terrorist: a person who uses extreme acts of violence to make a political statement or accomplish a political goal

Further Reading

Burgan, Michael. *George Bush*. Minneapolis: Compass Point Books, 2004.

Gormley, Beatrice. *President George W. Bush: Our Forty-third President*. New York: Aladdin Paperbacks, 2001.

Hughes, Libby. *George W. Bush: From Texas to the White House*. New York: Franklin Watts, 2003.

Kachurek, Sandra J. *George W. Bush*. Berkeley Heights, NJ: Enslow Publishers, 2004.

Schlesinger, Arthur M. Jr., et al., editors. *The Election of 2000 and the Administration of George W. Bush*. Philadelphia: Mason Crest Publishers, 2003.

MORE ADVANCED READING

Andersen, Christopher. *George and Laura: Portrait of an American Marriage*. New York: William Morrow/HarperCollins Publishers, 2002.

Bush, George W. *A Charge to Keep*. New York: Morrow, 1999.

———. *We Will Prevail: President George W. Bush on War, Terrorism and Freedom*. New York: Continuum, 2003.

Mansfield, Stephen. *The Faith of George W. Bush*. New York: Jeremy P. Tarcher/Penguin, 2003.

Schweizer, Peter, and Rochelle Schweizer. *The Bushes: Portrait of a Dynasty*. New York: Doubleday, 2004.

Woodward, Bob. *Plan of Attack*. New York: Simon & Schuster, 2004.

Places to Visit

Ameriquest Field at Arlington
(formerly the Ballpark at Arlington)
1000 Ballpark Way
Arlington, TX 76011
(817) 273-5222
http://texas.rangers.mlb.com/NASApp/mlb/tex/ballpark/tex_ballpark_history.jsp

George W. Bush was part of the ownership group of the Texas Rangers baseball team from 1989 to 1998. The stadium, originally called the Ballpark at Arlington, opened in 1994.

George H. W. Bush Presidential Library
1000 George Bush Drive West
College Station, TX 77845
(979) 691-4000
http://bushlibrary.tamu.edu/

The library, on the campus of Texas A&M University, is devoted to the life and work of President George H. W. Bush, who was the president of the United States from 1989 to 1993. It includes information about George W. Bush's early life with his family in Texas and many family photographs.

Texas Governor's Mansion
1010 Colorado
Austin, TX 78701
Visitors' Info Line: (512) 463-5516
http://www.txfgm.org/

George and Laura Bush lived in the Texas Governor's Mansion from 1995 to 2001. A virtual tour is available online.

The White House
1600 Pennsylvania Avenue NW
Washington, DC 20500
Visitors' Info Line: (202) 456-7041
http://www.whitehouse.gov/

George and Laura Bush took up residence in the White House in 2001.

Online Sites of Interest

★ **Internet Public Library, Presidents of the United States (IPL POTUS)**

http://www.ipl.org/div/potus/gwbush.html

Includes links to information about George W. Bush the man and about his presidency, including his speeches and several Internet biographies.

★ **Grolier: The American Presidency**

http://ap.grolier.com

Brings together material from five different Scholastic encyclopedias to provide background and context on the past, present, and future of the American presidency. Includes audio and video footage of the presidents dating back to Grover Cleveland.

★ **The White House**

http://www.whitehouse.gov

Provides an archive of President George W. Bush's speeches, press conferences, and more.

★ **September 11 News**

http://www.september11news.com

A comprehensive site about the September 11, 2001, terrorist attacks on the United States. Provides newspaper and magazine covers, news archives, photos of the attacks, and much more.

★ **Operation Enduring Freedom/Operation Iraqi Freedom**

http://www.globalsecurity.org/military/ops/enduring-freedom.htm

http://www.globalsecurity.org/military/ops/iraqi_freedom.htm

These sites provide a detailed overview of Operation Enduring Freedom, which resulted in the overthrow of the Taliban in Afghanistan in November 2001 and of Operation Iraqi Freedom, the invasion of Iraq in April 2003.

★ **Defend America**

http://www.defendamerica.mil

News and information from the U.S. Department of Defense about the war on terrorism.

Table of Presidents

	1. George Washington	2. John Adams	3. Thomas Jefferson	4. James Madison
Took office	Apr 30 1789	Mar 4 1797	Mar 4 1801	Mar 4 1809
Left office	Mar 3 1797	Mar 3 1801	Mar 3 1809	Mar 3 1817
Birthplace	Westmoreland Co, VA	Braintree, MA	Shadwell, VA	Port Conway, VA
Birth date	Feb 22 1732	Oct 20 1735	Apr 13 1743	Mar 16 1751
Death date	Dec 14 1799	July 4 1826	July 4 1826	June 28 1836

	9. William H. Harrison	10. John Tyler	11. James K. Polk	12. Zachary Taylor
Took office	Mar 4 1841	Apr 6 1841	Mar 4 1845	Mar 5 1849
Left office	**Apr 4 1841•**	Mar 3 1845	Mar 3 1849	**July 9 1850•**
Birthplace	Berkeley, VA	Greenway, VA	Mecklenburg Co, NC	Barboursville, VA
Birth date	Feb 9 1773	Mar 29 1790	Nov 2 1795	Nov 24 1784
Death date	Apr 4 1841	Jan 18 1862	June 15 1849	July 9 1850

	17. Andrew Johnson	18. Ulysses S. Grant	19. Rutherford B. Hayes	20. James A. Garfield
Took office	Apr 15 1865	Mar 4 1869	Mar 5 1877	Mar 4 1881
Left office	Mar 3 1869	Mar 3 1877	Mar 3 1881	**Sept 19 1881•**
Birthplace	Raleigh, NC	Point Pleasant, OH	Delaware, OH	Orange, OH
Birth date	Dec 29 1808	Apr 27 1822	Oct 4 1822	Nov 19 1831
Death date	July 31 1875	July 23 1885	Jan 17 1893	Sept 19 1881

5. James Monroe	6. John Quincy Adams	7. Andrew Jackson	8. Martin Van Buren
Mar 4 1817	Mar 4 1825	Mar 4 1829	Mar 4 1837
Mar 3 1825	Mar 3 1829	Mar 3 1837	Mar 3 1841
Westmoreland Co, VA	Braintree, MA	The Waxhaws, SC	Kinderhook, NY
Apr 28 1758	July 11 1767	Mar 15 1767	Dec 5 1782
July 4 1831	Feb 23 1848	June 8 1845	July 24 1862

13. Millard Fillmore	14. Franklin Pierce	15. James Buchanan	16. Abraham Lincoln
July 9 1850	Mar 4 1853	Mar 4 1857	Mar 4 1861
Mar 3 1853	Mar 3 1857	Mar 3 1861	**Apr 15 1865•**
Locke Township, NY	Hillsborough, NH	Cove Gap, PA	Hardin Co, KY
Jan 7 1800	Nov 23 1804	Apr 23 1791	Feb 12 1809
Mar 8 1874	Oct 8 1869	June 1 1868	Apr 15 1865

21. Chester A. Arthur	22. Grover Cleveland	23. Benjamin Harrison	24. Grover Cleveland
Sept 19 1881	Mar 4 1885	Mar 4 1889	Mar 4 1893
Mar 3 1885	Mar 3 1889	Mar 3 1893	Mar 3 1897
Fairfield, VT	Caldwell, NJ	North Bend, OH	Caldwell, NJ
Oct 5 1829	Mar 18 1837	Aug 20 1833	Mar 18 1837
Nov 18 1886	June 24 1908	Mar 13 1901	June 24 1908

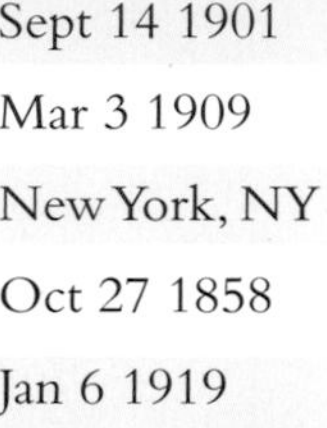

	25. William McKinley	26. Theodore Roosevelt	27. William H. Taft	28. Woodrow Wilson
Took office	Mar 4 1897	Sept 14 1901	Mar 4 1909	Mar 4 1913
Left office	**Sept 14 1901•**	Mar 3 1909	Mar 3 1913	Mar 3 1921
Birthplace	Niles, OH	New York, NY	Cincinnati, OH	Staunton, VA
Birth date	Jan 29 1843	Oct 27 1858	Sept 15 1857	Dec 28 1856
Death date	Sept 14 1901	Jan 6 1919	Mar 8 1930	Feb 3 1924

	33. Harry S. Truman	34. Dwight D. Eisenhower	35. John F. Kennedy	36. Lyndon B. Johnson
Took office	Apr 12 1945	Jan 20 1953	Jan 20 1961	Nov 22 1963
Left office	Jan 20 1953	Jan 20 1961	**Nov 22 1963•**	Jan 20 1969
Birthplace	Lamar, MO	Denison, TX	Brookline, MA	Johnson City, TX
Birth date	May 8 1884	Oct 14 1890	May 29 1917	Aug 27 1908
Death date	Dec 26 1972	Mar 28 1969	Nov 22 1963	Jan 22 1973

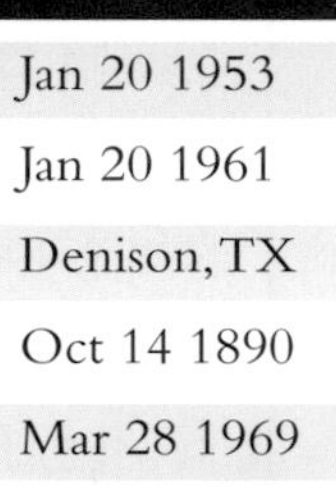
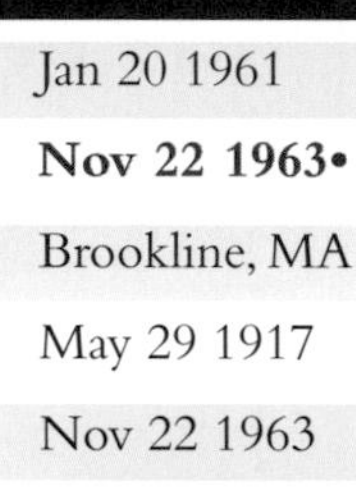

	41. George Bush	42. Bill Clinton	43. George W. Bush
Took office	Jan 20 1989	Jan 20 1993	Jan 20 2001
Left office	Jan 20 1993	Jan 20 2001	—
Birthplace	Milton, MA	Hope, AR	New Haven, CT
Birth date	June 12 1924	Aug 19 1946	July 6 1946
Death date	—	—	—

29. Warren G. Harding	30. Calvin Coolidge	31. Herbert Hoover	32. Franklin D. Roosevelt
Mar 4 1921	Aug 2 1923	Mar 4 1929	Mar 4 1933
Aug 2 1923•	Mar 3 1929	Mar 3 1933	**Apr 12 1945•**
Blooming Grove, OH	Plymouth, VT	West Branch, IA	Hyde Park, NY
Nov 21 1865	July 4 1872	Aug 10 1874	Jan 30 1882
Aug 2 1923	Jan 5 1933	Oct 20 1964	Apr 12 1945

37. Richard M. Nixon	38. Gerald R. Ford	39. Jimmy Carter	40. Ronald Reagan
Jan 20 1969	Aug 9 1974	Jan 20 1977	Jan 20 1981
Aug 9 1974★	Jan 20 1977	Jan 20 1981	Jan 20 1989
Yorba Linda, CA	Omaha, NE	Plains, GA	Tampico, IL
Jan 9 1913	July 14 1913	Oct 1 1924	Feb 6 1911
Apr 22 1994	—	—	June 5 2004

• Indicates the president died while in office.

★ Richard Nixon resigned before his term expired.

Index

Page numbers in *italics* indicate illustrations.

About the Author 

Matt Donnelly enjoys the opportunity to write about living history. He has written many articles for young readers and a biography of President Theodore Roosevelt. He was born in Massachusetts, but he now lives in Maine with his wife, daughter, and three cats.